Ministry and the Law:

What You Need to Know

Mary Angela Shaughnessy, S.C.N., J.D.

PAULIST PRESS
New York/Mahwah, New Jersey

Cover design by James F. Brisson

Library of Congress Cataloging-in-Publication Data

Shaughnessy, Mary Angela.
    Ministry and the law : what you need to know / by Mary Angela Shaughnessy.
        p.   cm.
    Includes bibliographical references.
    ISBN 0-8091-3789-5 (alk. paper)
    1. Clergy—Legal status, laws, etc.—United States—Popular works. 2. Ecclesiastical law—United States—Popular works. I. Title.
    KF4868.C44S53   1988
    349.73′088′2—dc21   97-44065
                                                                     CIP

Published by Paulist Press
997 Macarthur Boulevard
Mahwah, New Jersey 07430

Printed and bound in the
United States of America

Contents

Dedication

I dedicate this work, with great love, to my father,

Edward M. Shaughnessy, Jr.
(1921–1985)

He was a man of faith and courage, friend to all, devoted husband, loving father who was the anchor of my life and a role model for his six children. Truly, the Scripture words may be said of him, "He went about doing good." May we all do the same.

Acknowledgments

To all who have aided me in my work in the area of civil ministry and the law, I offer sincere appreciation. I wish to recognize some special people.

First, I wish to thank Maria Maggi, my editor at Paulist Press. Her encouragement of my efforts on behalf of law and ministry, and her support of this text, are deeply appreciated.

I offer thanks to my friends and colleagues at Spalding University in Louisville, Kentucky, where I am privileged to serve. Their constant support is deeply appreciated. I owe a special debt of gratitude to Dr. Thomas Oates, President, for his unfailing support and his willingness to keep in his employ a woman who is constantly "on the road" presenting seminars and workshops. Words cannot express the depth of my appreciation to Dr. Oates.

Miriam Corcoran, S.C.N., of Louisville, Kentucky has given untiring service as proofreader and editorial advisor for this text and for all my work. I owe her much gratitude.

My deep appreciation is always with those who have shared their lives in ministry with me by participating in classes and workshops throughout the country. I thank Edwin McDermott, S.J., and Mary Peter Traviss, O.P., of the Institute for Catholic Educational Leadership at the University of San Francisco, where I am privileged to serve as visiting professor. Their faith in my ministry is a constant source of encouragement.

Finally, I thank you, the readers. May God bless you and your ministry abundantly.

—*Mary Angela Shaughnessy, S.C.N., J.D., Ph.D.*
Louisville, Kentucky
May 1997

CHAPTER ONE

Introduction and Pre-Test

Not so very many years ago, people would have viewed the idea of lawsuits against churches and/or institutions sponsored by religious organizations as a virtual impossibility. Even if someone had brought a lawsuit against a church, one would expect the suit to be dismissed. People simply did not sue churches and their ministers.

But today's ministers cannot rest in the assurance that since they are doing God's work, they are immune from litigation. Lawsuits unheard of in the 1950s are now commonplace. Religious institutions and their staffs are particularly vulnerable to lawsuits and may be viewed as appropriate defendants to sue since the combined wealth of the churches they represent can be tapped to pay any judgments against them. Today's ministers, therefore, must have a working knowledge of civil law and how it impacts ministry.

The following ten-statement pre-test provides readers with an opportunity to assess their current knowledge of civil law and its governance of religious ministry.

Pre-Test

✎ Please mark the following statements TRUE or FALSE:

_____ 1. Persons in private institutions such as churches do not have the same rights they would have if they were in public institutions.

1

_____ 2. Handbooks and brochures promoting programs can be considered contracts.

_____ 3. Since adults can be held responsible for accidents occurring to children and adolescents under their care, persons under the age of 18 should never be left unsupervised.

_____ 4. Volunteers are not held to the same degree of legal responsibility as are paid staff.

_____ 5. Because of the doctrine of separation of church and state, churches and other religious organizations are not bound by discrimination law.

_____ 6. Since the possibility of allegations of abuse always exists, ministers should never be alone with persons under the age of 18.

_____ 7. Civil employment law can apply to the employment of individuals in church-related institutions.

_____ 8. Abuse of persons must involve some type of physical contact.

_____ 9. Ministers can be held liable for a young person's sexual harassment of another.

_____ 10. Ministers, both ordained and non-ordained, are permitted to keep confidential any information which is revealed to them in the ministerial setting.

Answers and Explanations

The answer to the first statement, *Persons in private institutions such as churches do not have the same rights they would have if they were in public institutions,* is *true.* Some readers, perhaps most, will be surprised to learn this. Yet, the laws governing the rights of persons in public and private sectors are very different. The most basic difference lies in the fact that persons in the public sector are protected by the United States Constitution, while those in the private sector are not and must depend upon contract law to delineate and protect their rights.

For example, a minister overseeing a program for young people would probably not allow an individual to wear a button proclaiming that women have the right to have an abortion. Such an expression of opinion, while constitutionally protected in the public sector, can be forbidden in the private sector. The First Amendment to the U.S. Constitution protects the free speech rights of citizens in the public sector in which individuals can criticize authority or policy without fear of retribution. Indeed, courts have issued injunctions demanding that government permit the free expression of ideas so long as the expression poses no immediate threat of harm to persons.

The private sector, by contrast, is free to set whatever parameters it deems appropriate for behavior, since persons choose to participate in the private sector, and can end that participation at any time. This topic will be discussed in greater detail in the next chapter.

Statement #2, *Handbooks and brochures promoting programs can be considered contracts,* is *true.* Contract law is the main source of the law affecting private institutions, including church-related institutions and programs. In the absence of any document that clearly states that it is a contract, courts will consider the provisions of any document that may confer contractual responsibilities and benefits. Handbooks are one of the main types of contractual documents found in the private setting. At its simplest, a contract is an agreement between two parties in which each party *receives* a benefit and each party *incurs* a detriment.

Some persons mistakenly believe that since church participation is voluntary, no rules can be enforced. On the contrary, church officials can enforce standards of behavior and can make adherence to those standards a contractual obligation. Chapter Two will develop the concept of contract law in greater detail.

Statement #3, *Since adults can be held responsible for accidents occurring to children and adolescents under their care, persons under the age of 18 should never be left unsupervised,* is *false.* There are times when a reasonably prudent person would leave young persons unattended because of some pressing necessity. The statement could be made true by adding the words, "without direction," to the end of the statement. Courts expect that children and adolescents will have been told what they are to do if no adult is present. Since most emergencies do not offer enough time for direction-giving, adult supervisors should make sure that those they supervise have been well-instructed concerning proper behavior in the absence of adults.

Accidents occurring when supervisors are absent constitute one of the greatest sources of negligence cases. The concept of negligence will be discussed in Chapter Three.

Statement #4, *Volunteers are not held to the same legal degree of responsibility as are paid staff,* is *false.* The law requires that individuals who accept responsibilities, regardless of the level of compensation they receive, are held to the same standards as those who are paid for their services. Sometimes administrators will express a belief that, since volunteers are unpaid and can choose to volunteer or not, there is little that can be done in terms of requiring certain levels of performance. This belief is mistaken. Those who administer programs are charged with, at minimum, the provision of a safe environment staffed with competent persons. Thus, the administrator can, and indeed, must set standards for all who work in the program and must supervise volunteers as carefully as paid staff. Chapter Four will present some guidelines in the selection, training, and supervision of volunteers.

Statement #5, *Because of the doctrine of separation of church and state, churches and other religious organizations are not bound by discrimination law,* is *false.* While the Constitution does not apply to the operation of churches and their ministries, statutes and regulations do. Discrimination law is statutory in nature, as it has been established by the legislature. While religious organizations are generally permitted to discriminate on the basis of religion, all other discrimination law can apply to churches and their programs. In fact, some developing case law indicates that when persons who possess a different religious belief or no religious belief are accepted as participants or staff members, the religious organization cannot discriminate against them on the basis of their sincerely held religious beliefs. Chapter Five contains a detailed analysis of the various aspects of discrimination.

Statement #6, *Since the possibility of allegations of abuse always exist, ministers should never be alone with persons under the age of 18,* is *false.* In the atmosphere of mistrust and accusation that ministers sometimes experience, the temptation is to avoid any possible problem area. While such an approach is certainly understandable, it may not always be in the best interests of the individuals involved. Obviously, a priest is not going to invite a third party in to witness a confession. A youth minister from whom a distraught teenager seeks advice would probably find it very difficult to give that advice if someone else had to be present for the conversation.

What is needed is a prudent approach. Private conversations should not be held in out-of-the-way, secluded places. If a minister is conducting a counseling session, he or she should be sure that: (1) others are in the general area; or (2) the door to the room is slightly ajar; or (3) some window(s) provide visual access to persons. Such actions are appropriate, yet respectful of the privacy needs of others.

Statement #7, *Civil employment law can apply to the employment of individuals in church-related institutions,* is *true.* Depending on the circumstances, civil employment law often governs employment decisions in private as well as public institutions. All institutions are expected to deal fairly with employees, even if they do not have to grant the full panoply of Constitutional protections.

Statement #8, *Abuse of persons must involve some type of physical contact,* is *false.* The realities of physical and sexual abuse are all too recognizable in today's society, but emotional and psychological abuse are types of abuse which may or may not have a physical component. Clergy, counselors, religious educators, and other ministers have powerful roles to play. Psychological and emotional abuse can be just as damaging as physical abuse, particularly when inflicted by persons in positions of trust.

The responsibility to report abuse is serious for those who work with persons under the age of 18 and/or with persons considered vulnerable adults, and the law establishes both reporting procedures and sanctions for failure to report.

Statement #9, *Ministers can be held liable for a young person's sexual harassment of another,* is *true.* Although such cases have been largely confined to the school setting, the potential certainly exists for young persons to sexually harass other young people in religious settings. Courts have also indicated a willingness to hear cases alleging negligent supervision by religious officials in instances in which one young person has sexually abused a younger child. Hence, the importance of knowing and being able to act in accordance with child abuse reporting laws cannot be overstated.

Statement #10, *Ministers, both ordained and non-ordained, are permitted to keep confidential any information which is revealed to them in the ministerial setting,* is *false.* The only two privileges left in the law are attorney/client and clergy/penitent. At least one state does not recognize clergy/penitent privilege. There is a strong historical tradition of respect for sacramental confession. Generally, courts will not seek to compel priests or other members of the clergy to reveal confidential information, although some statutes specifically mention that the privilege applies only to clergy in religions which recognize sacramental confession. There is no counselor or educator privilege recognized in the law at present. Issues regarding confidentiality will be discussed in Chapter Five.

This brief introductory pre-test should give the reader some idea of the complex and broad nature of civil law as it impacts religious ministry. While the already very busy minister may wonder why the law has suddenly become such an important factor in ministry, it is good to remember that Jesus himself recognized the importance of civil law when he said, "Render unto Caesar the things that are Caesar's and unto God the things that are God's" (Mt 22:21; Mk 12:17; Lk 20:25).

CHAPTER TWO

Sources of Law Impacting Ministry

Constitutional Law

Constitutional law is one of the major sources of civil law affecting public sector behavior in the United States today. Cases arising in schools provide some of the best examples of this fact. In the majority of public school student and teacher dismissal cases, for instance, plaintiffs allege deprivation of Constitutional rights. Ministers are probably familiar with certain Constitutional rights. The First Amendment guarantees freedom of speech, press, assembly, and religion; the Fourth Amendment protects against unlawful searches and seizures; the Fifth and Fourteenth Amendments guarantee due process.

Persons in public institutions, such as public schools, can claim Constitutional rights because a public school is a government agency and its administrators are government employees. The Constitution protects persons from arbitrary governmental deprivation of their Constitutional freedoms. However, persons in Catholic schools or other programs sponsored by the Catholic Church cannot claim such protections because private institutions administered by private persons are not governed by Constitutional protections.

These restrictions may seem somewhat unfair; yet a similar price is paid by anyone who works in a private institution. If a person goes to work in a gas station, the individual will probably be required to wear a uniform. The employee will probably not be permitted to wear a button advertising a different gasoline company, and so on.

The bottom line is that, when one enters a private institution, such as those sponsored by the Catholic Church, one voluntarily surrenders the protections of the Constitution. The individual is always free to leave, but, so long as the person remains in the institution, Constitutional protections are not available. Therefore, the Catholic Church and its program administrators and ministers do not have to accept behaviors about which public sector institutions have no choice and even are required to protect.

In short, what cannot lawfully be done in a public institution may be done in a church-sponsored one. For example, the First Amendment to the Constitution protects persons' rights to free speech; therefore, administrators in public programs may not make rules prohibiting the expression of an unpopular viewpoint. Most educators have heard of the landmark *Tinker* case which produced the now famous line, "Students and teachers don't shed their Constitutional rights at the [public] schoolhouse gate" *Tinker v. Des Moines Independent School District* 393 U.S. 503 (1969). Since no such Constitutional protection exists in religious schools and programs, administrators may restrict the speech of both participants and staff. Free speech issues in church programs rarely reach courts.

The United States Supreme Court ruled in 1985 in *New Jersey v. T.L.O.* 105 S.Ct. 733, that public school officials may use a reasonableness, rather than a probable cause, standard in conducting searches of young people. Religious institutions and programs are not bound by this case; however, common sense and Gospel respect for students as persons should govern searches in church-sponsored programs.

Public organizations must be concerned with Constitutional issues. Catholic institutions and programs, while not bound to grant Constitutional freedoms per se, are bound to act in a manner characterized by fairness. Some legal experts talk about a "smell" test. If an action "smells" wrong when a person examines it, it may be legally suspect. In the end, the actions expected of church-based programs and ministers may appear much like Constitutional protections. In no area is this more evident than in due process considerations.

Due Process Issues

The Fifth Amendment to the Constitution guarantees that the federal government will not deprive someone of "life, liberty, or property without due process of law." The Fourteenth Amendment made the Fifth Amendment and all other Amendments in the Bill of Rights applicable to the states. Persons entitled to Constitutional due process have substantive due process rights, property interests (that which can be the subject of ownership, including jobs and education) and liberty interests (freedom, reputation). Substantive due process involves moral as well as legal ramifications: is this action fair and reasonable? Substantive due process applies whenever property or liberty interests can be shown.

The Constitution also guarantees procedural due process, i.e., *how* a deprivation occurs. In the public sector, procedural due process includes: *notice* (a presentation of the allegations against the accused); *hearing* (an opportunity to respond) *before an impartial tribunal;* opportunity to *confront* and *cross-examine* accusers; and the opportunity to call *witnesses in one's own behalf.* In serious cases, a person in the public sector has the right to have an attorney present.

Churches and church-sponsored programs, while not bound to provide the whole panoply of procedural due process protections that the public sector *must* provide, are nonetheless expected to be fair. An Ohio court, ruling in a Catholic school discipline case, stated that courts could intervene in private school disciplinary cases, if "the proceedings do not comport with fundamental fairness." *Geraci v. St. Xavier High School* 13 Ohio Op. 3d 146 (Ohio, 1978).

Fundamental fairness in a Catholic school, program, or activity is akin to, but not synonymous with, Constitutional due process.

Statutory Law

Federal and state statutes and regulations, many of which have Constitutional bases, comprise a second source of the law affecting Catholic ministers. If a statute requires that all who operate an educational institution, a non-profit institution, or a church-related institution within a given state follow a certain directive, both private and public institutions are bound. So long as what is required does not unfairly impinge upon the rights of the private institution (such as a church) and can be shown to have some legitimate purpose, Catholic institutions can be compelled to comply with state and federal legislative requirements.

The only situation in which a Catholic institution or program can be required to grant federal Constitutional protections occurs when state action can be found to be so pervasive within the institution that the institution can fairly be said to be acting as an agent of a state. The key factor in state action is the nexus or relationship between the state and the challenged activity. Although litigants have alleged state action in Catholic schools, for example, no court of record has found state action present. In a 1982 private school teacher dismissal case, *Rendell-Baker v. Kohn* 102 S.Ct. 2764, the Supreme Court ruled that such a dismissal in a private institution which received 90–99% of its funding from the state did not constitute state action. *Rendell-Baker* seems to render the state action issue moot in cases alleging violation of Constitutional due process protections in private institutions.

A different situation exists in cases alleging violations of federal anti-discrimination and civil rights legislation. In such cases, the presence of federal funding can result in an institution's being required to abide by the legislation. Discrimination issues will receive more detailed consideration in Chapter Five.

Both historically and presently, churches and religious programs are not bound to grant Constitutional protections. It is very important for ministers to keep this in mind, as parents, young people, other parishioners, and employees sometimes claim that their Constitutional rights have been violated when, in fact, no Constitutional rights existed in the first place. These realities may need to be clarified very early in a relationship between a parish or a parish-sponsored program and its staffs, participants, and the parents of participants. One way to prevent possible misunderstandings is to develop and disseminate handbooks or program guides which outline the rights and responsibilities of all persons in the ministerial setting.

Common Law

A third source of the law affecting religious ministry is common law, which is case law determined by court proceedings and handed down through the ages. Commonly accepted standards of morality, such as the Ten Commandments and the "golden rule," are also considered part of common law. *Black's Law Dictionary* (1979), the definitive guide to definitions of legal terms, defines common law as follows:

> "Common law" consists of those principles, usage and rules of action applicable to government and security of persons and property which do not rest for their authority upon any express and positive declaration of the will of the legislature (p. 251).

The United States legal system was founded on the Anglo-Saxon system of law. Lawyers and judges search for precedents not only in the cases decided in the United States, but also in cases tried in English law before the United States established its independence as a sovereign country. Since case law involving religious institutions and ministry has increased substantially in the last ten years, there is a developing area of common law principles relating to ministry.

Contract Law

The prevailing law in religious institutions and ministry is contract law. A contract is an agreement between two parties who both incur detriments and derive benefits from the contract.

A youth minister, for example, agrees to provide youth ministry services at a parish. The minister could be considered to incur detriment in that one is unable to perform other employment during that time. At the same time, he or she receives a benefit, such as a salary, pension, etc. The parish, too, incurs both a detriment (payment of salary) and a benefit (young people are being provided services).

The young person who comes to youth ministry programs agrees to abide by the program rules, a type of detriment, and receives the benefits of participation. Likewise, a person who seeks counseling from a priest is entering into a kind of contract, even if no exchange of money is involved. The counselee agrees to be present for sessions, to abide by certain standards of appropriate counseling behavior, etc., and receives the benefit of counseling. The priest incurs a detriment in terms of time and a benefit of providing a service. It is important to keep in mind that oral contracts can be binding ("I will see you at 3:00 P.M. on Tuesday," and "I will be there") and do not necessarily involve monetary considerations.

BREACH OF CONTRACT

Breach of contract occurs when one party fails to perform. When a parish is involved in litigation with personnel, the court will examine the provisions of the contract. *Weithoff v. St. Veronica School*, 210 N.W. 2d 108 (Mich. 1973), an early

but significant case, illustrates this point. The parish termi-
nated Weithoff's contract after her marriage to a priest who
had not been laicized. She had signed a contract of employment
which bound her to observe the "promulgated" policies of the
sponsoring parish. A policy requiring teachers to be practicing
Catholics had been adopted by the governing body; the policy
was filed but never published to the teachers. Therefore, Ms.
Weithoff alleged that the parish's dismissal of her was a breach
of contract. The court agreed and ordered the parish to pay
damages (the remedy for breach of contract in the private sector is damages, not reinstatement).

Weithoff illustrates the importance of contract language. Had
there been no clause requiring "promulgation," there is a strong
possibility that the parish would have won this case; the court
might well have maintained that a person who teaches in a
Catholic school should expect to be held to the requirements of
church law.

Breach of contract can be committed by either party to the
contract. If a parish wrongfully terminates the employment of a
staff member, the individual could be awarded damages. On the
other hand, if an employee decides to break a contract, courts
tend not to award damages to employers, since it is generally held
that replacement staff can be found. Thus, no substantial damage
is sustained by the parish.

Program participants can allege failure to receive promised services. Several cases involving religious schools have made such
arguments, and the day is probably not far off when individuals
might claim that they were unfairly denied First Communion or
Confirmation or marriage within the church. However, it should
also be noted that traditionally courts have practiced the doctrine
of "judicial restraint" and have declined to become involved in dis-
putes that are doctrinal in nature because of the principle of separation of church and state.

Canon Law

Although canon law, church law, is obviously not part of the code of civil law, it is respected by the courts as evidenced by the "judicial restraint" doctrine cited above. A court will, nonetheless, intervene in matters that are within its purview, such as employment law, even if the intervention violates some principle of canon law.

CHAPTER THREE

Types of Lawsuits

The most common type of lawsuit is the tort, defined by *Black's Law Dictionary* as: "[a] private wrong or injury, other than breach of contract, for which the court will provide a remedy in the form of an action for damages" (p. 1335). This chapter will discuss several types of tort cases, including malpractice, abuse, and defamation of character. Negligence cases, however, constitute the bulk of tort cases in religious settings, so the concept of negligence will be considered first.

Negligence

Even though negligence is the "fault" against which ministers and religious administrators must guard, it is also one of the most difficult types of case about which to predict an accurate judicial outcome. What may be considered negligence in one court may not be considered negligence in another. It is much better, obviously, to avoid being accused of negligence in the first place than to take one's chances on the outcome of a lawsuit.

Since negligence is an unintentional act or omission which results in injury, a person charged with negligence is generally not going to face criminal charges. Persons who bring successful negligence suits are usually awarded money damages in an amount calculated to compensate for the actual injury suffered. It is possible, though rare, for a court to award punitive or exemplary damages if the court is shocked by the negligent behavior. In assessing whether a person's behavior is negligent, a court will use the "reasonable person" test: would a reasonable person [minister] in the defendant's situation have acted in this manner? "Reasonable" is whatever the jury or other fact-finder decides it is.

Courts also rely on the principle, "The younger the child chronologically or mentally, the greater the standard of care." Ninth-grade participants in Confirmation programs or 12th-grade students on retreat, for example, would not ordinarily require the same level of supervision that kindergarten students need.

Some people believe that children and teenagers can never be left unattended. Such a belief is mistaken. Courts recognize that emergencies can arise and that students might be left alone while the supervisor is taking care of the emergency. Judges expect, however, that supervisors will have told the young people previously, such as at the beginning of the term and periodically thereafter, what they are supposed to do if the supervisor has to leave. At minimum, rules might require that students remain in their seats when no adult is present. Parish administrators and ministers should consider developing a staff rule that young persons are not to be left unattended unless absolutely necessary, and that proper procedures are to be followed in the event of an emergency.

Youth ministry, religious education programs, counseling, and other ministerial settings present many possible negligence situations. In programs in which volunteers sometimes substitute for the regular minister, the supervising volunteer may not even know the young persons' names. He or she may not be skilled in dealing with young people. Pastors, other administrators, and ministers should insist that all persons who supervise young people, even substitutes, participate in an orientation in which appropriate skills can be addressed.

ELEMENTS OF NEGLIGENCE

There are four elements which must be present before legal negligence can be found: *duty, violation of duty, proximate cause, and injury.* If any one of these elements is missing, legal negligence cannot be present.

Duty

The person charged with negligence must have had a *duty* in the situation. Persons are not responsible for injuries occurring at a place where or a time when they had no responsibility. A pastor or youth minister walking through a mall on a weekend does not have a legal duty to parishioners who also happen to be at the mall. Within the religious or ministerial setting, however, students have a right to safety and clergy, other ministers, counselors, religious educators, and others have a duty to protect the safety of all those entrusted to their care.

One situation that presents problems from a negligence standpoint is that of the young person who arrives early for a religious activity and/or is not picked up at dismissal time. All staff must understand that young persons must be supervised from the time they arrive at the program site until the time they depart. If parents are late picking up their children, an adult staff member must remain with the students until the parents arrive. Pastors and other administrators must understand that the parish can be held liable for accidents that occur on parish property, particularly when the time of the accident is close to the beginning or end of an activity. Some people mistakenly believe that they can announce that no supervision will be provided and thus avoid liability. The legal theories stating that property owners are responsible for injuries occurring on their property apply in these situations. Since the young person had a legitimate reason for being present (even if he or she has arrived early or stayed late), courts will hold parishes and their administrators to the highest possible standard.

Another issue related to injury on parish property is presented by the trespasser or the person who has no legitimate purpose on the property. For example, consider a group of students who gather on parish property at eleven o'clock at night to "hang out." If someone is injured, a pastor could argue that he should not be expected to provide security for persons who come onto parish property at unauthorized times. Yet, the law demands that a property owner protect even trespassers from known hazards. Thus, if two young people begin fighting and an injury results, the parish will probably not be held liable. But if a person is injured as a result of some hazardous condition on the property, the parish could be held liable, as the administrators should have provided protection and/or warning for anyone who might enter the property.

The 1967 New Jersey school case of *Titus v. Lindberg*, 228 A.2d 65 illustrates the extent to which administrators can be held liable. In *Titus* the principal was found negligent and responsible for student injury occurring on school grounds before school hours because: he knew that students arrived on the grounds before the doors were opened; he was present on campus when the students were present; he had established no rules for student conduct outside the building, nor had he provided for student supervision. The court ruled that the principal had a reasonable duty to provide such supervision when he knew students were on the property before school opened.

It should be easy to see how a situation similar to that in *Titus* could arise in a ministerial setting or a religious education program. Who will supervise the early arrivals and the late pick-ups? This dilemma might well be taken to the supervising board for the development of a policy statement. Courts expect some policy as to when young persons may arrive at a program site, what rules they are to follow, and what kind of supervision will be provided.

In every situation, common sense has to prevail. Textbook solutions are rarely available for persons working with young people.

For example, a counselor who realizes on her way home that she has left an article at the parish and returns to retrieve it could discover that a ten-year-old is outside waiting for a ride and no other adult is present on the premises. The reasonable person would wait with the child until parents arrive or until some other transportation arrangement can be developed. The counselor may think that it is not her responsibility because she normally would not even be on the premises; however, a court could well decide that the point is that she was there and should have behaved in a professional manner. In the situation just described, a counselor or other minister may be tempted to put the child in her car and take him or her home. However, should a counselor do so and an accident occur, the counselor would be liable.

Violation of Duty

Negligence cannot exist if the second element, *violation of duty,* is not present. Courts understand that accidents and spontaneous actions can occur. If a minister is properly supervising young persons during a break and one individual picks up an object, throws it, and thus injures another, the minister is not responsible. However, if a minister who is responsible for supervision were to allow object-throwing to continue without attempting to stop it and a person were injured, the minister would probably be found to have violated a duty.

Similarly, a catechist who leaves a classroom unattended to make a personal, non-emergency telephone call will usually be found to have violated a duty if a student is injured and it can be shown that the catechist's presence could have prevented the injury. Moreover, if it can be shown that catechists often left students unattended while the Director of Religious Education (DRE), through inaction or inattention, did nothing about the situation, the DRE may have violated a duty as well. Under the legal doctrine of *respondeat superior* (let the superior answer), pastors and other administrators are often held responsible for the actions of subordinates. In determining whether the superior is liable, courts pose questions such as these: has the superior developed a clear policy for staff conduct in dealing with situations such as the one which resulted in injury? Has the supervisor implemented the policy? Are staff members supervised?

Proximate Cause

The violation of duty must be the *proximate cause* of the injury. The court or jury has to decide whether proper supervision could have prevented the injury and, in so deciding, the court has to look at the facts of each individual case. Proximate cause is not necessarily synonymous with direct cause. For example, in the object-throwing instance cited above, the student throwing an object would be the direct cause of the injury; however, the catechist's failure to intervene in the situation would be the proximate cause of the injury.

A well-known case which illustrates the concept of proximate cause is *Smith v. Archbishop of St. Louis,* 632 S.W.2d 516 (Mo. Ct. App. 1982). A second-grade teacher kept a lighted candle on her desk every morning during the month of May. She gave no special instructions to the students regarding the dangers of lighted candles. One day a child, wearing a crepe paper costume for a play, moved too close to the candle and the costume caught fire. The teacher had difficulty putting out the flames and the child sustained serious physical and resultant psychological injuries.

The trial court ruled that the teacher's act of keeping the lighted candle on her desk was the proximate cause of the child's injury. The court discussed the concept of *foreseeability;* it was not necessary that the teacher have foreseen the particular injury but only that a reasonable person should have foreseen that *some* injury was likely. The concept of foreseeability is important. Would a reasonable person foresee that there is a likelihood of injury? Religious education and youth ministry programs contain the potential for injuries like the one in *Smith.* Whenever possible, teachers and ministers should find alternatives to having open flames from candles. If lighted candles are used, extreme caution is in order.

Proximate cause is a complex legal concept. Religious education and youth ministry programs pose special dangers because participants are not in the traditional school setting. Young people's energy can stimulate their taking risks that could expose them to dangers. Pastors and other administrators would be wise to hold regular staff meetings to discuss the program, expectations, and foreseeable problems. These matters can then be analyzed in the light of health and safety requirements.

Injury

The fourth element necessary for a finding of negligence is *injury*. No matter how irresponsible the behavior of an individual, there is no legal negligence if there is no injury. If a youth minister leaves twenty young persons unattended for thirty minutes for no legitimate reason and no one is injured, there is no negligence in a legal sense. In order to bring suit in a court of law, an individual has to have sustained an injury for which the court can award a remedy.

In developing and implementing policies for supervision, the minister must ask, "Is this what one would expect a reasonable person in a similar situation to do?" The best defense for a minister or administrator in a negligence suit is a reasonable attempt to provide for the safety of all through appropriate rules and regulations.

Because of the seriousness of the dangers posed by religious education and youth ministry programs, a greater standard of care will be expected of DREs, catechists, and youth ministers than would probably be required of teachers in the traditional school setting.

Thus, ministers must take an offensive approach with regard to the elimination of hazards. All activities should be carefully monitored. All staff, both paid and volunteer, should receive thorough and ongoing orientation and instruction. The reasonable minister who supervises staff and practices prevention by constantly striving to eliminate foreseeable risks will avoid costly lawsuits and injuries.

Clergy Malpractice

The concept of malpractice is well-known, although it is commonly associated with lawsuits against doctors and lawyers. In recent times, the concept has been broadened to include malpractice by many types of professionals, including clergy and other ministers.

Black's Law Dictionary (1990) offers the following definition:

> Professional misconduct or unreasonable lack of skill. Failure of one rendering professional services to exercise that degree of skill and learning commonly applied under all the circumstances in the community by the average prudent reputable member of the profession with the result of injury, loss or damage to the recipient of those services or to those entitled to rely upon them. It is any professional misconduct, unreasonable lack of skill or fidelity in professional or fiduciary duties, evil practice, or illegal or immoral conduct (p. 959).

As Black's definition illustrates, anyone can allege clergy or ministerial malpractice by attempting to prove either a lack of competence to perform appropriate duties or a willful decision to perform such duties badly. Counseling presents one such situation in which malpractice can easily be asserted. The counselee can claim that the priest or other minister practiced therapy without a license or certification. The line between pastoral listening, spiritual direction, and psychological analysis or psychiatric treatment can be hard to define. A person who has been talking on a regular basis with a priest may find that his or her depression or anxiety has increased; he or she may then decide to "make the priest pay" for this ongoing state of unease. No one can take responsibility for the "cure" of another person's troubled mind or spirit, but it is important for a minister to set parameters during initial sessions and to recommend referral to a trained professional, such as a psychologist, psychiatrist or other physician, or social worker, as appropriate. If it is clear that no progress is being made in a counseling situation and the person will not accept a referral, the minister may have to terminate the relationship.

Alleged sexual abuse claims often include an accusation of malpractice. The topic of sexual abuse will be addressed in detail in Chapter Five. For now, it is sufficient to note that sexual abuse is a special type of malpractice.

There have been some allegations of failure to impart the true teachings of the Catholic Church. The author learned of at least a few court cases which alleged that ministers had failed to instruct parishioners in the magisterium of the Church. In one such unpublished case, a Catholic school teacher alleged that teaching according to the texts and curricula prescribed by the Church had caused her to lose her faith! While such a case may seem outrageous, it does indicate the signs of the times. Ministers are vulnerable to lawsuits for everything they do. It is best to recognize these realities, and to practice preventive law; by understanding the minimum requirements of the law, a minister is better able to comply with those requirements.

Child/Vulnerable Adult Abuse

One of the great social concerns of our times is the issue of child abuse, whether mental, physical, psychological, or sexual. Society in general, both inside and outside the Catholic Church, abhors child abuse.

In the past several years, increasing numbers of states have added the classification of "vulnerable adults" to those who can be considered victims of criminal abuse under the law. One accepted definition of vulnerable adult is "a person eighteen years of age or older, who due to impairment of mental or physical function or emotional status, is unable or unlikely to report abuse or neglect without assistance." Persons with mental disabilities of any kind, including young adults with conditions formerly referred to as types of mental retardation and older adults suffering from geriatric senility and/or Alzheimer's disease, can be classified as "vulnerable adults."

Clergy and other ministers are in particularly sensitive positions. Young persons, and to a lesser extent vulnerable adults who can still communicate, often choose ministers as their confidants in dealing with abuse and its effects. Therefore, pastors and other church administrators and supervisors must ensure that all staff members are as prepared as possible to deal with the realities of abuse and neglect. Pastors and supervisors should spend time reviewing pertinent state law and church/program policies and providing time for discussion.

STATUTORY CONSIDERATIONS

All fifty states have laws requiring the reporting of suspected abuse and/or neglect. Ministers are almost always considered mandated reporters, a term which means that persons so designated *must* report suspected child abuse.

While statutory wording can vary from state to state, the statute will ordinarily require, as does the state of Kentucky, that a mandated reporter "who knows or has reasonable cause to believe that a child [or vulnerable adult] is an abused or neglected child [or vulnerable adult], shall report or cause a report to be made in accordance with the provisions of this section" (KRS 199.335(2).

Statutes generally mandate reporting procedures. The mandated individual usually makes an oral report, followed by a written one within a specified period of time, often 48 hours.

Statutes usually provide protections for a person who makes a good faith report of child abuse which is later discovered to be unfounded. Such a good faith reporter will not be liable to the alleged abuser for defamation of character. However, a person can usually be held liable for making what is referred to as a "malicious report," one which has no basis in fact and which was made by an individual who knew that no factual basis exists. Conversely, statutes usually mandate that a person who knew of abuse or neglect and failed to report it can be fined and/or charged with a misdemeanor or felony.

DEFINING ABUSE

What is abuse? It is sometimes defined as, "Corporal punishment gone too far." That definition may seem to apply only to abuse of children, but there are also well-documented cases of beating of the elderly. Excluding, of course, sexual abuse, the definition appears to have merit. However, it also raises questions: How far is too far? Who makes the final determination? Can what one person considers abuse be considered valid parental corporal punishment by another? Are there any allowances for differing cultural practices? It is difficult to give a precise definition that will cover all eventualities. Certainly, some situations are so extreme that there can be little argument that abuse occurred. A young person who appears at a parish function with cigarette burns has been abused by someone, even if the injuries are self-inflicted. When a person alleges sexual abuse, however, there probably exist only two conclusions: (1) the child is telling the truth, or (2) the child is lying. In some cases, there is a third possibility: the person is mistaken in believing that he or she has been sexually abused. The investigating agency, not the reporter, will have to determine which conclusion is the true one. Ministers, teachers, counselors, volunteers, and others must understand that they are the reporting agents, not the screening agents.

The majority of cases will probably not be crystal clear and a minister may struggle in making a determination as to whether a report must be filed. Many law enforcement officials and some attorneys advise persons to report everything that they are told that could possibly constitute abuse. Again, it is not the job of the reporter to determine if the abuse has occurred. Appropriate officials will decide whether the report should be investigated further or simply "screened out" as a well-intentioned report that does not appear to constitute abuse.

TRAINING STAFF AND VOLUNTEERS

Pastors, administrators, and others with supervisory responsibilities should provide staff members, paid and volunteer, with inservice training concerning the indicators of child/vulnerable adult abuse and neglect, as well as the legal procedures for reporting such conditions. There are many excellent resources available. Local police departments, abuse hot lines, and social service agencies are usually happy to make both materials and speakers available for inservice presentations. Some of the most helpful materials identify warning signs or situations that should alert persons to possible abuse.

WHO SHOULD FILE A REPORT?

Some experts argue that the administrator should make all child abuse and/or neglect reports so that the same person is reporting all situations in a given setting. Although individual state laws vary, all require that the person with the suspicion either make the report or cause a report to be made. Inservice presentations must stress that this requirement is legally binding on the person who suspects the abuse, not on that person's supervisor. If a staff member files a report, his or her supervisor should be notified that such a report has been made. It is legally dangerous for the parish and/or other institution or program if, when a police officer or other official appears to investigate a report of abuse, the pastor or other administrator does not know that a report has been filed.

Pastors and program administrators, in conjunction with school principals as appropriate, should decide in advance how visits and requests from police and social workers will be handled. Many states now require that educational personnel, for example, allow officials to examine and question students without staff persons present. Clergy and other ministers should seek legal counsel in determining the applicable laws and procedures in a given state.

STAFF MEMBERS AND ABUSE

It is well established that schools and religious settings attract persons with abusive tendencies who are seeking young people upon whom to prey. Thus, it is important that administrators do everything in their power to investigate the background of persons before they begin work as paid or volunteer staff members. This topic will be discussed in greater detail in Chapter Four.

Defamation of Character

"Can I be sued for what I say about a person?" is a question often asked by ministers and staff who want to do the right thing for those to whom they minister but who want to protect themselves as well. The simple answer to the question is, "Yes, you can be sued." Ministers are wise to be concerned about what they and other staff members say. Some basic information may prove helpful in establishing a philosophical and practical framework for statements made about the people entrusted to one's care.

WHAT IS DEFAMATION?

Defamation is a type of tort, a civil wrong. Persons who bring defamation suits will have their claims heard in civil, not criminal, courts. Persons who allege defamation seek money damages, not the criminal convictions of the person(s) who defamed them. Defamation of character involves twin torts: slander, which is spoken, and libel, which is written. Defamation is an unprivileged communication, i.e., a statement made by one person to a third party who is not privileged to receive it.

In any ministerial setting, a court might well inquire as to the necessity for the communication. If the communication is found to be unnecessary, even if true, the court could find the individual charged to be, in fact, guilty of defamation.

Black's Law Dictionary (1979) defines a defamatory communication: "A communication is defamatory if it tends so to harm the reputation of another as to lower him in the estimation of the community or to deter third persons from associating or dealing with him" (p. 375).

Some people mistakenly believe that the truth is an absolute defense to defamation. Persons who work with children and adolescents, or persons holding positions of public trust, such as in ministry, are generally held to a higher standard than is the average adult in a defamation suit. When a minister repeats confidential information about a person, the defense of truth may not be sustained because the minister holds a position of trust and, thus, can be held to a higher standard than the ordinary person. Ministers must ensure, then, that opinions and facts concerning those they encounter in the ministerial setting are stated only to those having a right to know.

Any documentation concerning persons must be both accurate and protective of the rights of individuals whose behavior is being described. Records must be objective and factual. Communications should be measured against the standard, "What is written should be specific, behaviorally-oriented, and verifiable." It is better to say,

"Mr. Smith did not appear for his last three counseling sessions. On the previous two occasions when he was present for the sessions, he appeared preoccupied, drew pictures on a note pad, failed to answer several questions, and stated that all priests are weird." Such a record is better than stating, "Mr. Smith usually forgets his sessions. When he does come, he is not interested, refuses to focus, and states unfounded, bizarre opinions." The less personal opinion that is stated about an individual, the better.

SLANDER

Slander, or oral defamation, can arise in seemingly innocent situations. For example, staff rooms have long been considered safe places in which adults can express themselves freely. So long as the only persons present in the room are staff members, one may speak without fear of being accused of slander. It is generally held that staff members are people with a "right to know" the thoughts and perceptions of other staff members.

Social gatherings may present other problems. A parent may come to a youth minister at a neighborhood party and state, "My son has been spending a great deal of time with Bobby X. I am not so sure that Bobby is a good influence. What is your opinion?" If the youth minister responds, "I don't think Bobby is a good influence either," he or she could be found guilty of defamation of character, unprivileged derogatory communication. Ministers should avoid even the appearance of defamatory speech and, hence, should avoid giving opinions concerning persons they encounter in their ministry to those who have no real right to know those opinions.

All persons working in ministry should be extremely prudent in making any comments, whether oral or written, about people. All should remember that a person has a right to reputation. Ministers should treat the reputations of those entrusted to their care with at least as much care as they would want their own reputations to be treated.

LIBEL

Libel, written defamation, is generally easier to prove than is slander. Ministers must be sure that the comments made in records or in other documents are based on verifiable occurrences rather than on conjecture, as indicated above.

Questions often arise concerning situations in which ministers are asked to write recommendations for persons. Obviously, if the writer wishes to praise a person, the likelihood that the person could object is minimal. The problem occurs when a minister cannot, in conscience, write a favorable recommendation. The minister then has two possible courses of action. He or she can refuse to write a recommendation; after all, no one has an absolute right to a recommendation. Some, however, may feel uncomfortable refusing requests for recommendations. The minister or catechist may then opt for a general letter of reference which does little more than verify that the minister does know the individual and that the individual participated in some ministry or service or program. This kind of letter says nothing derogatory about a person, although it certainly says nothing very positive, either. The individual receiving the letter should be able to tell that the letter does not constitute an overwhelming endorsement of the person.

The annals of church history contain many stories of persons who have committed acts which may render them unsuitable for ministry, but who, nonetheless, have been given favorable recommendations and obtained subsequent ministerial positions. Giving a person a positive recommendation when one is not warranted can result in liability under the tort theory of negligent recommendation. Thus, extreme caution is in order. The appropriate question is not, "How can I write so that I won't get sued?" but, "How can I write so that I protect both the reputation of those in my care and my own reputation as a minister who abides by the highest ethical standards?"

The Catholic Church and Discrimination Law

Federal anti-discrimination law can bind Church-related institutions. Anti-discrimination law is statutory, enacted by legislatures, and so governs the Catholic Church in ways that Constitutional law cannot. Most Catholic schools routinely file statements of compliance with federal anti-discrimination laws with appropriate local, state, and national authorities. It is almost unheard of for a Catholic school or religious education program to be accused of discriminating in regard to students. Unfortunately, it is not as uncommon to hear of alleged discrimination concerning personnel.

Discrimination can be defined as treating persons of a certain group in a different manner because of some group characteristic. The Catholic Church cannot discriminate on the basis of race, sex, color, national origin, age, and disability (if, with reasonable accommodation, the needs of the disabled person can be met so that the disabled person can still perform job requirements). Sex can be used as a condition of employment only if certain positions have a long tradition of being held only by members of one sex; an obvious example is priestly ordination. Since the Catholic Church has approximately two thousand years of a male clergy, it is unlikely that any U.S. court would find the Church guilty of sex discrimination because it acts in accordance with its own tradition and teaching.

The Catholic Church can discriminate on the basis of religion, and Catholic teachers *can* be given preference in hiring. Ministers and others responsible for the administration of parish programs must exercise caution and avoid even the slightest suggestion of inappropriate discrimination.

The 1980 Catholic school case, *Dolter v. Wahlert,* 483 F.Supp. 266 (N.D. Iowa 1980) is instructive. Ms. Dolter, an unmarried teacher in a Catholic school, became pregnant. The principal later rescinded her contract, although evidence indicated that although he knew that certain *male* faculty members had engaged in premarital sex, he had taken no action against *them*.

The court rejected a "separation of church and state" defense and ruled that the issue in this case was not the Church's prohibition against premarital sex, but rather was sexual discrimination. Anti-discrimination legislation can impact the Catholic Church and its ministries because the government has a compelling interest in the equal treatment of all citizens. The *Dolter* court noted, however, that the non-renewal of the teacher's contract would have been upheld if males known to have engaged in premarital sex had been treated in the same manner. The problem, then, was not the school's prohibition of premarital sex, but the fact that rules had been unfairly applied on the basis of sex.

Age discrimination laws prohibit discrimination against persons who are 40 years of age or older. It is not permissible to ask potential employees their age prior to employment. It is not uncommon to find pastors and school principals who say, "I prefer to hire a DRE or a teacher right out of college or with little teaching experience. We can save money by not hiring more experienced people." True financial exigency can be a reason for choosing a less experienced applicant. If the applicant were to challenge the Catholic parish or school in court, it would be difficult to win the case based on financial exigency if arguably non-essential expenses were paid. For example, a principal who declined to hire a teacher based on "no money to pay" and who subsequently spent $50,000 on non-budgeted items for which there was no clear need might be found liable for age discrimination.

Disability discrimination law can pose challenges to the administrator/minister. Chapter Five will discuss the legal requirements in greater detail. What is important for the administrator/minister to understand is that a person cannot be denied employment or participation in a program simply because of the existence of a disability.

CHAPTER FOUR

Personnel Issues

"What can I legally do?" is an important question often asked by clergy and other ministers. It is crucial that ministers understand the basic parameters of the law, particularly in personnel matters. If there is any question of what the law permits, competent legal counsel should be consulted. It is wise to anticipate potential difficulties before one is faced with the reality of an actual problem. This chapter will discuss civil law and appropriate canonical considerations as they relate to personnel issues in Catholic institutions.

The last few decades have been times of great change for the Church. In less than thirty years, the majority of DREs and Catholic school teachers has shifted from members of religious congregations to lay people. Dioceses and parishes have had to confront the issues of paying just salaries to teachers, providing benefits, and developing legally sound policies and procedures. These issues have forced administrators to examine the legal soundness of actions and documents.

It is sometimes a struggle to match word with deed. The law is a parameter within which we operate. While the law is not the minister's reason for being, it does affect ministry. If a minister moves outside the legal parameters, everything inside the parameter can be jeopardized.

Canon law governs the existence of religious institutions and their relationships with various persons and institutions within the Church. Parishes, schools, and programs can begin and sustain institutional life only with the approval of the local bishop. All Catholic schools, for example, whether diocesan sponsored or not, are subject to the bishop in matters of faith and morals.

The Revised Code of Canon Law calls for subsidiarity and collegiality in relationships and structures within the Church. Subsidiarity requires that persons having disagreements or complaints should seek discussion and resolution of the problem at the level closest to the problem. The importance of following the principle of subsidiarity cannot be stressed too strongly. No one at any level of authority—from principal or DRE to pastor to diocesan administrator to the bishop—will take any action on a complaint until the person complaining has met with the individual most directly concerned. If this procedure became standard practice in ministry, an untold number of problems could be solved before major crises develop. Subsidiarity also helps to ensure that each person's authority in the hierarchy of Church government is protected.

Collegiality respects the competence of each person involved in a decision-making process. Persons committed to collegiality generally try to govern by consensus. Consensus does not necessarily mean that everyone agrees that a certain action is the best possible action; rather, consensus means that all members have agreed to support the decision for the sake of ministry. It is important to note that consensus does not mean that the minority agrees to go along with the majority; it means that all members can support a decision; sometimes, the majority will support the action that the minority favors.

Bishops, pastors, DREs, youth ministers, and principals attempting to follow the provisions of canon law will usually be upheld, if challenged in a court, because of the First Amendment's protection of freedom of religion. This protection is not absolute, as the case of *Reardon v. LeMoyne*, involving four women religious in conflict with the diocesan office, illustrates. The *Reardon* court found that civil courts, while not allowed to interfere in purely doctrinal matters, did have jurisdiction over the civil employment contracts of religious. The days of religious superiors' directing a religious to leave quietly and move on to a new assignment are over. Whatever rights are afforded lay personnel should be afforded clergy and religious as well. Of course, whatever rules govern personnel should also apply to employees who are clergy or members of religious communities. There is no room for a privileged class or a double standard in ministry, nor should there be such a contradiction of basic justice.

Pre-Employment Issues

Pastors and administrators want to hire the most qualified, suitable individuals they can find. Sometimes, in the zeal of the search, compliance with the law can be compromised. Two legal issues are paramount in hiring procedures: pre-employment inquiries and background checks.

Pre-employment inquiries carry the potential for violation of a person's rights. Administrators want to gather as much job-related information as possible, but at the same time invasion of privacy and impermissible inquiries must be avoided. There are several areas of impermissible inquiries: (1) questions concerning marital status and family status, although questions regarding being married in the Church are acceptable; (2) questions which are not job-related, regarding such areas as disability, national origin, etc.; and (3) age-related questions. It should be noted, however, that questions which are impermissible before employment may be asked after employment, since, once the applicant has become an employee, the questions are no longer the basis for hiring.

Questions related to an applicant's practice of the Catholic faith are permitted, since courts recognize that such questions concern the existence of a BFOQ, or "*bona fide* occupational qualification." Religious institutions are permitted to hire, or give preference to, members of the particular religion which they represent. Although one is legally permitted to do so, there is no requirement that a particular denomination hire only persons of that religious belief.

Pertinent job-related questions are allowed, such as, "Is there any condition or situation that may cause you to have a problem with regular attendance?" The existence of a disability in an applicant can be problematic for Church employers. Section 504 of the Rehabilitation Act of 1973 applies to institutions receiving any type of federal financial assistance. In the case of parishes with schools, such assistance has probably been accepted. Most Catholic schools receive lunch subsidies, block grant monies, or other forms of assistance. Some persons argue that such assistance is not significant; however, the costs associated with being the respondent in a test case would probably be monumental, as compared with the cost of compliance.

Section 504 of the Rehabilitation Act of 1973 states that a person cannot be denied employment simply because of a handicap. A handicapped or disabled individual is one who has a physical or mental condition that significantly affects one or more life functions such as movement, speech, sight, etc. Disabled persons must be given fair employment consideration if, with reasonable accommodation on the part of the employer, they can perform the duties of the position. Thus, a job application or an interviewer should not ask, "Do you have a handicap?" but rather, "Is there any physical or mental reason why you would not be able to perform the responsibilities of this position?"

Questions regarding arrests and criminal records must be worded carefully. A person may have been arrested but never convicted. Most attorneys recommend a question such as, "Have you ever been convicted of a crime involving moral turpitude?" Some examples could be given, such as rape, murder, and felony convictions involving injuries of any kind to another person. If a person answers Yes to such a question, he or she should be asked to give the details. It is advisable to state that conviction of such a crime is not an automatic bar to employment and that the hiring officials will consider the nature of the offense and the relationship between that offense and the position sought.

Applicants should be asked to sign a statement giving permission for background checks. Many states now have laws requiring that all persons who work with persons under the age of 18 be fingerprinted and the fingerprints be checked against records of felonies and/or misdemeanors. In the absence of such state law, a diocese may wish to set its own policy regarding fingerprinting.

Pastors and other administrators *must* check all references. Sometimes persons observe that an applicant will not give the name of an individual who will make negative comments about the applicant. However, references do occasionally give less than glowing recommendations and may be quite candid in their assessments. There also exists the possibility that a person's name may be listed as a reference without that individual's consent. Policy should require that all references be checked, and employment should not be finalized until they are.

Supervision and Evaluation of Personnel

Several recent research studies indicate that administrators consider supervision of staff a primary responsibility. However, many administrators readily admit that supervision ranks low in terms of the amount of time spent on the task. More immediate and seemingly more pressing concerns clamor for administrative attention. Yet, surely the supervision of employees has to be one of a pastor's, principal's, or other minister's most important legal and ethical responsibilities.

It is the administrator's responsibility to ensure that qualified personnel are employed. Pastors and other ministers must make decisions about employee performance. Those who serve in parish ministry in schools or other areas who do not leave voluntarily when they are found to be professionally deficient, should not have their employment continued if remedies for improvement have been exhausted. However, competent employees should find supervision and evaluation procedures to be a protection for them.

Often administrators find themselves struggling with the ethical as well as the legal dimensions of situations. No one wants to end the employment of individuals whose families' livelihood depends on their income; yet, justice demands that ministers be competent and caring.

NOT SYNONYMOUS TERMS

Supervision and evaluation are not synonymous terms. As most school principals learn in administrative preparation classes, supervision is a formative experience, whereas evaluation is a summative one. Practically speaking, supervision is the observation of employees in classrooms or other work situations. Administrators should make regular visits to classrooms, youth ministry sites, and so on.

Supervision can be problematic for both the administrator and the employee. A principal who never taught any grade lower than the sixth may feel inadequate in a first-grade teacher's classroom; a high school principal who taught English may feel less than competent in a physics classroom. A pastor may feel that supervising employment is not his area of expertise. Nonetheless, pastors and other administrators should be able to recognize good job performance within five to ten minutes of entering a classroom or other ministry site. If supervision is an ongoing process, both administrator and employee can grow together and help each other to improve the learning and/or ministerial setting. If supervision is seen as punitive—as something that is done only if the administrator is "out to get the employee"—it will not be successful.

Evaluation is summative: an administrator sums up all the available data and makes a decision regarding contract renewal or continuance of employment. Evaluation of performance should be based on more than supervisory data. The administrator will seek to answer such questions as, "Does this person support the rules of the parish, school, or program? Does he or she look after the safety of young people and/or others entrusted to the employee?" as well as, "Is he or she a good subject matter teacher or religious educator or youth minister or secretary?" Evaluation, then, is a more encompassing concept than supervision, but both should be present in an effective ministerial employment setting.

It is important to remember that teachers and other religious educators are in parishes for the good of those to whom they minister. Those who are entrusted to employees' care are not there for the minister's employment. There is no more serious legal responsibility than ensuring that parish programs are being staffed by capable, competent, caring employees and that all are encouraged and given the means to become the best they can be.

The importance of knowing what is expected of them cannot be underestimated. The staff or faculty handbook should contain a statement of the supervision and evaluation a staff member can expect. For example, who will supervise? How often? What, besides ministry/classroom observations, will form the basis for evaluation?

Supervision enables an administrator to make legally sound decisions about contract renewal and/or employment continuation. Declining to renew a contract or terminating employment seems unethical if the supervisor has never observed the employee on the job. Yet there are persons who have lost teaching positions, for example, because they "couldn't keep order" or were judged "incompetent," even though no formal supervision had ever occurred. Consistent, careful supervision ensures that persons are treated in appropriate legal and ethical ways.

EMPLOYEE PROTECTION

Supervision is also an employee's best defense against unjust termination. Should anyone allege that a minister is not doing an adequate job, the supervisor's observations can protect the employee. If a parent were to claim that a student now in the third grade could not read, for example, and the first- and/or second-grade teacher is to blame, it would be hard to prove the claim false if no professional had ever supervised the teacher(s). If, however, a supervisor could say, "I visited Mrs. Smith's class four times last year and students were being taught reading concepts. They were reading, and Mrs. Smith's lesson plans contained adequate time for the teaching of reading," it would be much harder, if not impossible, for an accusation to be supported.

Analogous situations exist in other ministerial settings. If a parent were to claim that a young person received inadequate preparation for Confirmation, leading the student to decline to receive the sacrament, supervisory data would be helpful. While such a situation may seem far-fetched, reports of just such complaints are beginning to surface in ministerial settings.

Non-Renewal Decisions

If a decision is made not to renew an employee's contract, administrators need to be clear about the individual's employment status. Public school teachers may have tenure ("an expectation of continuing employment"), while Catholic school teachers and other Church employees generally do not unless protected by a union contract. Catholic school teachers are usually employed under one-year contracts, as are other ministers. There is a growing tendency, however, to hire Church employees on an employment at will status without contracts. Such a decision should be carefully considered so that all ethical and pastoral issues have been adequately discussed. Church administrators should guard against situations which permit persons to view the parish or diocese as an unfair or capricious employer.

Non-renewal of contract and dismissal from employment are not synonymous terms. Non-tenured or non-contractual employees do not have the same rights as tenured teachers at the end of a given contract year. A non-tenured teacher may or may not be offered another contract, or another employee may be told at any point, in the absence of a contract, that employment will not be continued; there are no guarantees of ongoing employment. Of course, one should not lightly decide against renewal of the contract of a teacher or the continued employment of an individual who has been in the parish or school for a substantial number of years; a decision of non-renewal in such a case has ethical as well as legal ramifications. Nonetheless, a person who has a year-to-year contract or no contract should not be seen as having a legal expectation of continuing employment, unless that person can give credible evidence supporting such an expectation.

It is appropriate policy to state in the staff or faculty handbook or contract the reasons and procedures for termination and non-renewal of contract. Having written procedures can make everyone's positions clearer and can give all parties guidance in working through a termination.

Unless a staff handbook or contract states otherwise, a non-tenured employee does not have to be given the reasons for non-renewal of contract and/or non-continuation of employment. It might seem that the ethical action would be to give the person the reasons so that self-improvement might be sought. Problems can result, though, when an employee then attempts to prove in court that the reasons are either not true or insufficient. This is but one example of the kind of ethical and legal dilemma in which administrators can find themselves. In a way, administrators are involved in a kind of juggling act—attempting to balance the legal dimensions of one's position with the ethical issues. If, however, the administrator has supervised properly and kept appropriate documentation, a decision of non-renewal should not come as a surprise.

Administrators might find the following suggestions helpful:

1. develop a planned, orderly procedure for supervision of employees;
2. publish the procedure and give copies to all affected;

3. treat all employees consistently;
4. put records of observations and evaluations in writing in which the administrator:
   - confines him or herself to the facts
   - does not speculate on motivation or attitude
   - follows the rule: "If the administrator doesn't have to say it, it isn't said"
   - writes as though it is certain that others will read what is written.

DOCUMENTATION OF EMPLOYEE BEHAVIORS

Church administrators often ask questions concerning written documentation of employee behavior. Twenty years ago it was rare to find much written documentation in employment files. Administrators often expressed a belief that little or no documentation was good, since this procedure gave a person a second chance. Today, increasing litigation against administrators demonstrates that such a belief is not effective operational theory. On the contrary, documentation is an absolute necessity in protecting both institutions and administrators; complete documentation also ensures that employees' rights are protected. The next section will address some of the main issues in documentation, and will offer a model for record-keeping.

Contracts and Related Documents

The staff or faculty handbook and/or the employment contract should state, at least in general terms, the expectations for behavior. It is unfair for a teacher or staff member to be told, after the fact, that certain behavior is unacceptable if there are no standards, or if standards are vague. Obviously, there are some behaviors which everyone ought to know are unacceptable, such as theft, dishonesty, etc. The handbook and/or contract should also indicate what behaviors can result in termination of employment or in non-renewal of contract. The important factor to keep in mind in any such situation is documentation. The best protection against a successful lawsuit is a written record of the reasons and events leading to termination.

Some behaviors fall into "gray" areas. For example, what is inappropriate behavior with young persons? What is sexual harassment? Is it sexual harassment if the person is joking? (Answer: Yes! Chapter Five will provide more information.)

When an administrator believes that an employee has done something which is unacceptable, the administrator should ask whether the parish or school's documents state that such behavior is inappropriate. If there is any possibility that a reasonable person might not have known that such an action was prohibited, the administrator should do the following: give the employee the benefit of the doubt; advise the employee that such behavior is not acceptable, and that any such subsequent behavior will be documented; and immediately take steps to ensure that all employees are made aware of the parish or school's expectations.

The administrator should document all events that illustrate what it is that makes an employee ineffective or undesirable. Administrators should keep in mind that employees may be doing an adequate job in the ministerial or work setting, but may still be behaving outside the setting in ways that are unacceptable or that compromise effectiveness in the ministerial or school setting. Some examples might be: excessive absenteeism or tardiness, lack of cooperation, criticizing school, parish, or Church officials to young persons or others, etc. All documentation should be written in language that is specific, behaviorally-oriented, and verifiable. It would be better to record, "Mr. Thompson sent ten students to the DRE's office during a forty-five minute period" than, "Mr. Thompson is having difficulty keeping order."

In cases in which employee behavior does not meet administrative expectations, the supervisor should have a "paper trail" indicating that the employee was told of problems and given an opportunity to improve. One way to ensure appropriate communication and documentation is to follow a seven-point checklist when conferencing with employees who present problems.

Checklist for Conferencing with Employees

The following checklist can be used in drafting a document which is presented to the employee and in conducting the actual conference.

(1) *Enumerate precisely what is wrong and needs improvement.* Because it is difficult to correct other adults, administrators may fall into the trap of speaking too generally; the employee may not know exactly what he or she did that was not acceptable and may not understand what new behavior(s) are expected.

(2) *State that the parish or school wants the employee to improve.* Such a statement indicates good faith on the part of the administrator and can be most important in any subsequent litigation.

(3) *State what the parish or school is going to do to help the employee.* A beginning teacher or catechist could be assigned a more experienced teacher as a mentor who could advise in matters of instruction and classroom management. A teacher or catechist could also be sent to another parish or school for a professional day experience of observing instructors with proven records of effective teaching and discipline. A teacher with personal problems could be referred to a counselor.

(4) *Give a deadline at which time all parties will review improvement or lack thereof.* If no deadline is given and maintained, an employee could later claim, "I never heard back from you, so I assumed everything was all right." Thus, it is absolutely imperative that the administrator give

time parameters, such as two weeks, a month, two months; a date and time for a follow-up meeting should be established before the end of the conference.

(5) *Tell the employee that, if there is no improvement within the timeframe stated, disciplinary action will result.* Administrators may ask, "What sort of disciplinary action can I take?" An employee or volunteer can be put on probation, given notice of non-renewal, and/or suspended for a time period.

(6) *Give the employee a copy of the conference document stating the first five points and ask the individual to comment on the document to ensure understanding.* This procedure allows the employee the opportunity to ask for, and be given, clarification of any points.

(7) *Have the employee sign the document and add any comments he or she wishes to include; if the employee refuses to sign, have another person witness that fact.* This other person should be another administrator or the pastor; if neither is available, a secretary could serve as a witness. Asking a peer of the employee, such as a fellow teacher, should be avoided.

AVOIDING PROBLEMS

Although there is no foolproof formula for avoiding documentation problems, careful, objective recording of facts provides the best possible protection. Objective documentation lessens the possibility of misinterpretation and/or multiple interpretations. If an administrator writes, "Mrs. Jones has an attitude problem," one can ask, "What does that mean? An attitude about what? Students? Authority? The Church?" But if one writes, "Mrs. Jones refused to sign up for any of the religious education committees, refused to submit her records by the deadline, told students that rules governing playground behavior were 'stupid,'" the meaning is clear. Specific documentation enables the administrator to work with the employee in identifying strategies to improve behavior. Careful, accurate record keeping also protects an administrator against allegations of defamation, should the records ever be shared with a third party. It is hard to deny that one said playground rules are stupid, if there were witnesses; but it is easy to deny that one has an "attitude problem" or a "problem with authority."

PRACTICAL CONSIDERATIONS

Some administrators ask if every problematic employee behavior should be formally documented in an employee's personnel file. The answer is, "Not necessarily." For example, if an administrator notices that a teacher is five minutes late for class one morning, but has never been late before, the administrator may decide not to confront the teacher. However, an administrator might jot a note in his or her calendar or log book noting the tardiness. Whether the information would become part of a written personnel report would depend on whether subsequent problems occurred.

Problems and resentment can often be avoided if administrators ask themselves: Is this the fair thing to do? Is it moral? Is this the action I would want or expect someone to take if I were in the employee's position? Is it the position Jesus would take? Sometimes it is difficult to balance legal and Gospel issues, but such is the challenge facing Catholic administrators.

Volunteers in Ministerial Settings, Including Schools

Volunteers have served a valuable function in society for many years. Most Catholic school graduates will recall lunch room and library mothers as part of their own school experience. Today, the use of volunteers is growing in parishes and schools, and administrators are rightly concerned about utilizing volunteer service effectively while ensuring that legal considerations have been adequately addressed. The administrator should seek to ensure that only competent individuals are accepted as volunteers and that those accepted are given the information and help necessary to perform their tasks in a satisfactory manner. The following section will address some of the major concerns in the selection and training of volunteers.

NEGLIGENCE: A LAWSUIT WAITING TO HAPPEN

Every person reading this text has probably heard at least one story of a volunteer whose actions or inaction caused or exacerbated injury to a young person. Students certainly can be injured in settings in which no negligence occurred. However, negligence is the allegation most likely to be raised if an individual is injured while under the supervision of a volunteer.

If a volunteer is sued for negligence, the odds are fairly high that the supervisor will be sued as well, under the doctrine of *respondeat superior*, "let the superior answer." It is, therefore, extremely important that administrators develop policies and procedures for volunteers that ensure that all volunteers know what is expected of them.

A second type of negligence case can be brought against administrators. This type of case arises most often in situations alleging sexual abuse. The *volunteer* is not charged with negligence, but with some intentional tort such as sexual assault or rape. The volunteer's *supervisor* is then charged with negligence for failing to investigate properly the volunteer's background prior to accepting him or her in the parish or school setting. Thus, background screening of volunteers is imperative.

BACKGROUND SCREENING

Currently, two main types of background screening procedures exist. The first is the fingerprint check. As stated earlier, several states now have laws requiring that anyone who works with young people be fingerprinted. The fingerprints are sent to a state agency that checks them to determine if the person has a criminal record. The mere existence of a criminal record does not automatically make an individual unsuitable as a volunteer; the nature of the offense and the time elapsed since the offense should be considered. For example, a person with a record of sexual offense should never be allowed to work with young people. However, a person who has a twenty-year-old conviction for larceny but who has been rehabilitated may be acceptable.

The second type of background search involves checking references. Volunteers should be asked to complete an application and to give references. The administrator should ensure that the references are checked. Neither fingerprinting nor background checking is foolproof. However, each provides excellent data for use in assessing whether a person should be entrusted with young people. In the unfortunate event that a student injury does occur, the administrator and/or the pastor will be in a much sounder legal position if background searches have been made on persons who volunteer on a regular basis.

Should an injury occur and a lawsuit be filed, courts will consider the foreseeability of that injury. No one is expected to foresee everything that could possibly happen; but one is expected to foresee reasonable happenings and to take appropriate precautions. In the case of *Poelker v. Macon Community School District*, 212 Ill. App.3d 312, 571 N.E.2d 479 (1990), a student was hit by a discus thrown by another student during a warmup session which was supervised by an adult volunteer. The court, declining to find the volunteer liable for the injury, ruled "School district owed duty to participant to provide supervision during warmups." The supervision that is provided must be competent; if an adult volunteer is not familiar with an activity assigned for supervision, some instruction must be given so that foreseeable injuries can be avoided.

As indicated above, not every injury is foreseeable. In the case of *Bender v. First Church of the Nazarene*, 59 Ohio App.3d 68, 571 N.E.2d 475 (1989), a church was sued after a fourteen-year-old volunteer raped a six-year-old. The court, finding that such an event was not reasonably foreseeable, declined to find the church responsible.

A parish administrator can legitimately ask, "How practical is this information? Surely, we are not expected to run a background check on every parent who volunteers to chaperone a field trip." The likelihood that a court would expect background checks to be run on every parent who volunteers on an occasional basis is slim. In light of the exploding litigation in our society, however, the day of requiring background checks on any individual who intends to volunteer any service involving supervision of young persons may not be too far in the future. For the present, it seems that background checks should be done on any person who will be volunteering on a regular basis in situations in which young people are present. Such situations might include: serving as aides in religious education classes or youth ministry; cafeteria, playground, and classroom supervision; lunchroom monitoring; library presiding; computer room monitoring; and working alone with individual children or small groups of students.

Some educators may be concerned that parents and others will resent being subjected to background searches. The administrator who explains that this procedure is a standard one, undertaken to protect all children, should find the majority of potential volunteers understanding and cooperative. Those who do not wish to follow the procedure simply will not participate as volunteers.

TRAINING YOUR VOLUNTEERS: AVOIDING LITIGATION

The best way to avoid injury and subsequent litigation is to provide every volunteer with some inservice training. Such training need not be lengthy. Topics might include: (1) the parish, school, or program philosophy and goals; (2) the importance of volunteers in the setting; (3) duties of the volunteer; (4) discipline procedures, with a clear indication of when offending persons should be referred to a staff member; (5) health and safety measures; (6) duties specific to given activities, such as field trips; (7) an explanation of supervision as both a mental and physical activity.

It is not sufficient to be physically present with students; one must be mentally present as well. These facts mean that a volunteer cannot be engaged in doing something other than supervision. For example, volunteers should not be reading the newspaper or engaging in conversation with another volunteer or staff member while supervising students. Such activities, nonrelated to the supervisory function, could be problematic if a young person is injured and can demonstrate that the supervising volunteer's attention was not on the students.

Some individuals believe the myth that a volunteer cannot be "fired." The reality is that volunteers can, and sometimes should, be told that their services are no longer needed. If volunteers are incompetent or unwilling to meet reasonable expectations, their services should be ended. Following the documentation model presented above can be helpful in ensuring that any such termination of volunteer services is done in an appropriate manner.

Finally, an administrator may consider developing a volunteer handbook which would include the items listed above and any other information the administrator considers important. Protecting students and avoiding litigation are certainly goals of any Catholic administrator and/or minister. As in many other areas of professional concern, common sense is a helpful guide in the selection and training of volunteers. Asking how one would wish the volunteers supervising one's own children or other young relatives to be selected and trained is a means of ensuring sound policies.

A relatively recent case illustrates the principles discussed above. In the 1992 case, *Woodell v. Marion School District,* 414 S.E.2d 794 (S.C.App.), the guardian of a student injured when another student assaulted her at school during the school day brought suit against the school district for negligence. The complaint alleged that the school was grossly negligent in its supervision of both victim and assailant. The trial court granted the school's motion to dismiss the case, but the appellate court reversed the trial court's decision and remanded the case for trial. Referring to South Carolina law, the court stated, "A governmental [or other] entity may be liable to a student for a loss when the entity's responsibility to supervise, protect, or control a student is 'exercised in a grossly negligent manner.'" If a governmental entity can be held liable for gross negligence, a Catholic parish or school (private entity) can be held liable for gross negligence as well. Thus, all ministers must strive to provide adequate supervision for everyone in school and parish programs. Thus, administrators must adequately supervise all (professional staff and volunteer) who direct young persons.

CHAPTER FIVE

Special Topics

The preceding chapters have discussed fundamental issues of civil law that should be considered by anyone working in the area of church ministry. This chapter will deal with special topic areas that are also of grave importance in the administration of ministry.

Boundary Issues

Ministers, catechists and other staff members care about those to whom they minister. That care extends to other, arguably non-ministerial areas of life. For instance, ministers often find themselves counseling young people and others in personal matters; it is not unusual for ministers to find themselves in the position of "surrogate parent" for someone. Young people, in particular, often entrust ministers with confidential information. Ministers, many of whom are not trained counselors, often have questions about what is appropriate in interacting with students and clients outside the ministerial, classroom, and/or parish setting. There are few guidelines available; yet catechists and other personnel may deal with situations that pose personal and legal risks for themselves as well as for young people. The author is familiar with several situations in which parents threatened or pursued legal action against an educator or minister whose actions they viewed as unwise, inappropriate, sexually motivated, or interfering with the parent/child relationship. Thus, all adults working in the ministry of the Church should be aware of the legal ramifications involved in staff/client or teacher/student relationships.

CONFIDENTIALITY

Most educators and ministers rightfully consider student confidences to be sacred. If a student confides in a catechist, the student should be able to presume that the confidential information normally will not be shared with anyone. Educators, in turn, often believe that they have some type of immunity which protects them from legal liability if they refuse to share confidential information.

However, the facts indicate that very few states provide any sort of immunity or privilege for persons who receive confidential information from others. If a teacher or minister were subpoenaed, placed on the stand, and asked for confidential information, most judges would require the person to answer. Except in cases involving priests in sacramental confession, ministers do not have the privilege of refusing to answer questions asked under oath. Another situation that is fairly common involves the student who tells an adult that suicide or other violent action is being considered. Such information must be shared with appropriate persons or the adult who receives the confidence can risk being found liable for negligence if injury occurs.

To avoid misunderstanding, all educators and other ministers should establish the ground rules for confidences early in the relationship. Catechists or youth ministers who require journal writing or other exercises that may involve the sharing of personal feelings should inform the entire class of the rules. Basically, ministers should honor the confidences of others unless health or safety is involved; in such an instance, the confiding individual should know that the greater good requires that the information be revealed.

SEXUAL MISCONDUCT

One type of legal liability present in ministry is represented by sexual misconduct. Sexual misconduct *can* be alleged in apparently innocent situations. Persons *can* misinterpret touching, and ministers *can* find themselves facing child abuse charges. Caution is in order whenever any minister touches a person. This is not to suggest that all touching should be avoided. There are times when touch is appropriate and advisable—e.g., gestures of support, comfort, empathy—but there are other times and types of touch that are not appropriate. It is advisable to anticipate these kinds of situations before they occur. A pastor or other religious leader could gather staff members, volunteer as well as paid, and role play potential situations.

Another kind of problem is posed by a student who believes that a minister has not responded to efforts to achieve a closer relationship. Such a person may accuse a minister of inappropriate conduct as a retaliatory measure. Ministers must be aware that serious consequences can result from a claim of child abuse, even if the accusation is eventually proven to be false. At the very least, such a false allegation can be extremely embarrassing for the minister. If a child abuse report is made, the minister will be questioned by authorities and the investigation will be recorded. Some states even keep lists of suspected child abusers. Thus, it is imperative that ministers protect themselves and the persons to whom they minister by practicing appropriate behavior.

To avoid even the slightest hint of impropriety, a minister should, whenever possible, avoid being alone with a young person behind closed doors unless a window or other opening permits outsiders to see into the area. A good question to ask of oneself might be, "If this were my child, would I have any objection to a person relating with him or her in this manner?"

Fear of child abuse allegations has caused some public school districts in this country to adopt school rules that prohibit any faculty from touching a student. Such rules preclude putting one's arm around students, patting a student on the back, or even giving a student a hug. No Catholic ministerial administrator would want to take such a position, but common sense precautions nevertheless must be taken for the protection of all.

OTHER PHYSICAL CONTACT

Persons can also be charged with non-sexual child abuse. Corporal punishment, which is prohibited by statute or regulation in most schools, can set the stage for allegations of physical abuse. Corporal punishment can be defined as "any touching that can be construed as punitive." This author is aware of a case in which a teacher tapped a child on the shoulder with a folder while reprimanding the child for not having his homework done. The child's mother filed a child abuse report and threatened to file charges of assault and battery. Although this case is outrageous, it does indicate the dangers that can exist. Thus, administrators are well-advised to adopt an operating rule: "Never touch a child in a way that can be construed as punitive."

OTHER BEHAVIORS

All ministers and staff must keep in mind that they are professionals, or can be viewed as such, rendering a service. Just as a counselor or psychiatrist is professionally bound to avoid emotional involvement with a client, a minister should strive to avoid becoming so emotionally involved with a person that objectivity and fairness are compromised. Ministers must remember that they have many for whom they are responsible and who need and may desire the minister's attention. If a relationship with one individual keeps a minister from responding to other needs on a regular basis, the minister should seriously examine the appropriateness of the relationship.

In seeking to assess the appropriateness of a relationship, some mental health professionals recommend asking oneself questions such as these: Whose needs are being met? Is there a boundary? Where is it?

The following adult behaviors could be considered inappropriate, depending on the totality of the circumstances: dropping by a young person's home, particularly if no parent is present; frequent telephoning of the individual; social trips with an individual student; sharing of the minister's personal problems.

Serving as a Catholic minister in these times is a privilege and a gift. It is indeed sad when a minister is forced to relinquish that gift because of inappropriate choices. Thoughtful reflection and prudent behavior will keep ministers both legally protected and professionally fulfilled.

KEEPING CONFIDENCES: WHAT CAN YOU TELL? WHAT SHOULD YOU TELL?

One of the more perplexing situations facing ministers today is that presented by sharing of confidential information. The young persons of today may well face more pressures and problems than those of any other time. Broken homes, alcoholism and drug addiction, sexual and physical abuse, depression, and violence were certainly found in earlier eras, but they seem to be more prevalent, or at least more openly acknowledged, than they were when the majority of ministers were children and teenagers. The responsibility for receiving confidences and advising persons in both day-to-day situations and crises can be overwhelming. Busy ministers may well ask, "What am I supposed to do? I know I'm not a professional counselor, a psychiatrist, or a social worker, but I'm the one the person trusts, the one the individual has consulted. Are there certain legal issues involved in the receiving of confidences? Is there some information that must be made known to others, even when the person has asked for and received a promise of confidentiality from me?"

These are appropriate questions for any minister to ask. No one can afford to think that he or she can help all students all the time. If a student were to come to a teacher and tell the teacher he or she is experiencing shortness of breath and chest pain, the teacher would quickly summon both the student's parents and medical assistance. Yet, psychological problems are no less serious than physical ones, and the lay person who attempts to deal with such problems unaided may well be courting tragedy for both self and student. The next section will address the following specific topics: (1) confidentiality; (2) legal immunity of counselors; (3) journal writing; and (4) special situations such as retreats.

Confidentiality

Confidentiality is generally held to mean that one individual or a group of individuals will keep to themselves information that has been given to them. For example, the person who receives the sacrament of reconciliation rightfully expects that the subject matter of confession will be held sacred by the confessor and will not be revealed to anyone. Indeed, there are accounts of priests who have died rather than break the seal of confession.

Friends share confidences with each other. One individual may say to another, "This is confidential. You cannot repeat it." The person speaking in confidence has a right to expect that the confidant to whom the information has been given will keep the matter confidential. But there are recognized limits to what friends will keep confidential. For example, if one's friend confides that she has been stockpiling sleeping medication and plans to take all of it that evening so as to commit suicide, it is evident that morality requires that the confidant communicate such knowledge to a spouse or other family member of the confiding individual, or take some other action that would intervene in the attempted suicide.

It is not unheard of for a minister, who would not hesitate to help a friend who is threatening bodily harm to self or others, to believe that a young person who is talking about suicide is not serious, or can be talked out of the planned action, or is not capable of carrying out a threatened suicide. As child and adolescent psychologists report, young people do not usually comprehend the finality of death and do not think through the long-term ramifications of a suicide attempt. There is also, among some young people, a fascination with death, as can be seen by the idolization of famous people who have died young or committed suicide.

If a person tells a minister that he or she is going to harm self or others, the minister must reveal that information, even if a promise of confidentiality has been given. In a number of lawsuits brought against teachers and school districts, parents sought damages from teachers who were told by students in confidence that they planned to harm themselves or others; the teachers did not contact parents or other authorities. In some cases, the educators were held to be negligent in failing to warn the appropriate individuals.

Legal Immunity

It is a widely held myth that counselors, physicians, psychologists, and social workers have legal immunity from responsibility for any injuries that may arise from their not acting on confidential information presented to them. Most states have abolished counselor immunity, and the few who still "have it on the books" have imposed severe limitations on the concept. A counselor who hears from a young person that the individual plans to kill his or her parents and does nothing about it will not be legally able to decline to answer questions under oath, nor will the counselor be held harmless for any resulting injuries if he or she decides not to reveal the threats. Ministers and teachers must make it very clear to confiding individuals, as indicated in the section above, that they will keep their confidences *unless* their own health, life, or safety—or those of others—is involved.

The only two privileges from disclosure of confidential information which seem to remain in state law are that of priest/penitent and attorney/client. Even the husband/wife privilege, which allowed a spouse to refuse to testify against a spouse, has been largely abandoned.

In light of the above facts, a minister must presume that no legal protection exists for those who receive confidences. What should the minister do who wants to be a role model for young persons, who wants to be approachable and helpful? The answer is simple: Lay down the ground rules for confidentiality before you receive any confidences. Tell persons you will respect their confidences except in cases of life, health, and safety. If a person asks to talk to you in confidence, reiterate the ground rules before the sharing begins.

Journal Writing

Teachers of religion, language arts, English, and other subjects have long recognized the value of journal writing. Catechists, youth ministers, and pastoral counselors may also request persons to keep a journal. This practice does, however, carry a real risk of disclosure of information that the minister, counselor, or teacher will be compelled to reveal. All must set the same rules for confidentiality as are discussed above.

Adults must understand that they *are* expected to read what young persons write. If the adult does not intend to read such an assignment, then it should not be given. In particular, teachers and catechists should avoid such techniques as telling students to clip together pages they do not wish read or to write at the top of such pages, "Please do not read." Journal writing has a place in today's curricula and experiences, but supervising adults must be sure that young persons understand the parameters of the assignment and of the adult's responsibilities of reporting threatened danger.

Retreats

The retreat experience is extremely important for today's Catholic young people, as well as for adults. However, students are often at their most vulnerable in such situations. They may share stories of child abuse, sexual harassment, family dysfunction, even possible criminal activity. While encouraging students to share, the group leader must once again set the ground rules before the sharing begins. The use of peer leaders does not lessen the responsibility of the supervising adults. Peer leaders must be told of the ground rules and of the necessity to communicate them to group members as well as procedures to be followed in notifying adults if matter that must be reported is revealed in sessions.

RELEVANT CASE LAW

In *Brooks v. Logan and Joint District No. 2,* 903 P.2d 73 (1995), parents of a student who had committed suicide filed an action for wrongful death and a claim for negligent infliction of emotional distress against a teacher who had assigned the keeping of journals to her class.

Jeff Brooks was a high school student assigned to Ms. Logan's English class. Students were asked to make entries into a daily journal as part of their English composition work. For a period of four months prior to his death, Jeff wrote in his journal.

After his death, Ms. Logan read through the entries and gave the journal to a school counselor, who delivered it to Jeff's parents. Jeff had made journal entries which indicated that he was depressed and that he was contemplating suicide. One entry read as follows:

> Well, Edgar Allen Poe, I can live with studying about that stuff he wrote especially the one short story about the evil eye... I used to write poems until I pronounced myself dead in one of them and how could I write poems or stories if I was dead....
>
> Recently... see I went into a medium depression and wrote poems to two special people.... I told them it was too bad that I had to say goodby this way like that but, it would be the only way and I felt better....

Ms. Logan maintained that Jeff had requested that she not read his entries, so that he would feel free to express himself. The journal contained a note in which Ms. Logan stated that she would not read the journal for content, but would only check for dates and length. The parents maintained that, in a conversation with Ms. Logan after their receipt of the journal, she stated that she had "*re*read the entries." Ms. Logan later denied that she made that statement, and contended that she had not read the entries in question until after Jeff's death.

The lower court granted summary judgment in favor of the teacher and the school district. However, the appellate court reversed the finding, and held that there were issues of fact in existence which could only be determined at trial.

Thus, a trial court must determine whether Ms. Logan's actions or inactions constituted negligence contributing to Jeff's death. Part of the analysis will have to include a determination as to whether Jeff's suicide was foreseeable: Would a reasonable person in Ms. Logan's place have recognized the possibility of suicide and notified someone? The appellate court refers to case law in which jailers have been held liable for the suicide of prisoners when the prisoners had exhibited warning signs.

This case and the discussion in this section indicate the vulnerability of adults who receive student confidences. While the responsibility to adult clients is a bit less because of the age of the journal writers, threatened harm to self and others must still be reported. The wise minister, educator, or counselor will establish and enforce ground rules for dealing with confidences, and will seek help from supervisors and/or client's parents, family members, or friends, when appropriate.

Discrimination Revisited

Chapter Two discussed the concept of discrimination law and its applicability in ministerial settings. This section will address in greater detail the issue of religious discrimination and discrimination based on disability.

Churches and programs offered by churches are generally free from charges of religious discrimination, since the law recognizes that a church will give preference to members of its religion. Thus, Catholics may be given preference in hiring. Job descriptions may state that being a practicing Catholic is a requirement, or BFOQ (*bona fide* occupational qualification), as discussed in Chapter Four. There has been some suggestion, however, that once a religious organization has hired a non-member, accommodations to religion can be required if the job expectations have not been clearly explained prior to employment. For example, a Catholic school could require that all teachers attend religious services and supervise participants so long as that expectation has been stated as a condition of employment. If expectations are not clear from the onset, it is more difficult to enforce them. The Equal Employment Opportunity Commission has heard cases from Catholic school employees who were not Catholic and who alleged religious discrimination and demanded an accommodation of their beliefs.

The question of appropriate lifestyle for a practicing Catholic raises other issues. There is no definitive statement as to what constitutes a practicing Catholic, and reasonable minds differ. It is perhaps easier to list behaviors that would *not* be considered appropriate to a practicing Catholic. What is clear is that the Catholic Church and other religious groups can require adherence to the directives of the religion. So, if a person divorces and remarries without an annulment, a parish can terminate the employment. If the person is living an openly gay lifestyle, that person's employment may be ended. If the person is living with a member of the opposite sex and the arrangement is a source of scandal, that individual can be dismissed. The church administrator must bear in mind, however, that there can be some instances in which an unmarried person can live with a member of the opposite sex and there is no apparent wrongdoing. Trying to determine which realities are cause for termination can be confusing. This author recommends that administrators not engage in witch hunts; that is, rather than try to ferret out the truth of situations, deal with what comes to your attention and make decisions based on scandal or potential scandal.

DISABILITY DISCRIMINATION

As stated earlier in Chapter Four, the Rehabilitation Act states that a person cannot be denied employment simply because of a disability. Disabled people must be given fair employment consideration if, with an employer's reasonable accommodation, they can perform the duties of the position. Employers should note, however, that giving fair employment consideration does not mean that disabled persons must be hired; it does mean that they cannot be excluded from employment *solely* because of a disability that could be reasonably accommodated.

STUDENT/PARTICIPANT SPECIAL NEEDS

It is not uncommon for pastors and other ministers to receive inquiries from parents of religious education/youth ministry students as to how the parish or program will meet the disability needs of their children who want to participate in programs. Since persons with special needs are as much children of God as anyone else and since discrimination law can protect them, it is a good practice to be proactive rather than reactive in determining policies and procedures in this area.

Section 504 of the Rehabilitation Act of 1973 and the 1992 Americans with Disabilities Act (ADA) can seem to be legal quagmires. While there is an exemption in the ADA for churches, the court system is still sorting through cases to determine what exactly the exemption means. Myths and half-truths abound. Some consultants and lawyers have advised pastors and principals that schools must be made totally accessible. Many administrators fear that the cost of accommodation will be so high as to force schools and programs out of existence. Other administrators question accepting students with special needs. Can the average Catholic school or religious education program provide the proper adjustments needed by these students? Church personnel need a clear understanding of legal requirements.

Catholic institutions are not required to meet every need of every child. Most Catholic schools and religious education programs are not equipped to offer educational services to everyone. While a religious education program is not required to institute a special program, with special teachers, for a blind student or a profoundly mentally handicapped student, courts are indicating that such programs should be available somewhere, such as in a neighboring parish or at a diocesan center.

Neither Section 504 of the Rehabilitation Act of 1973 nor the Americans with Disabilities Act requires that institutions create programs to meet the needs of the disabled. What these laws require is that institutions not discriminate against persons who are seeking admission to their programs. If a disabled person can participate in the program with a reasonable amount of accommodation, then the institution must provide the accommodation. If providing that support system would create a significant hardship, the institution will not have to provide it. For example, if a blind student were to seek admission, and acceptance of that student would require that a special teacher be employed for the student and that all teachers learn Braille, the parish would probably not be expected to incur those expenses, yet it would be expected to find an equivalent education or program at a reasonably located site.

It must be frankly stated, however, that simply because one is not legally required to do something, it does not follow that one should not do that thing, if it is the *right* thing to do. If a parish could afford a sign language interpreter, or procure a volunteer one, to assist with a deaf student or to instruct the faculty and staff in signing, the administrator may have a moral and ethical duty to provide for the student even though the law does not require such provision. Indeed, the Pastoral Statement of U.S. Catholic Bishops on Handicapped People (1978) seems to demand such action: "If handicapped people are to become equal partners in the Christian community, injustices must be eliminated." Certainly, parishes should be leaders in fighting injustice wherever it is found, especially as it affects those whose disabilities place them among those for whom Christ manifested special concern.

Much apprehension could be alleviated if administrators clearly understood what the law does and does not require. In the final analysis, though, the question is not, "Did you do what you had to do?" but, "Did you do what you should have done?"

Sexual Harassment

Today's minister has probably heard much about sexual harassment. Newspapers carry stories of alleged sexual harassment and resultant lawsuits. No longer is sexual harassment something that is found only between two adults or between an adult and a child. School children claim that they have been harassed by peers. The news stories can seem overwhelming, and the potential for legal liability great. What, then, can the minister do?

Administrators should first ensure that they understand what sexual harassment is. It is commonly defined as "unwanted, unwelcomed, uninvited sexual conduct." Title VII of the Civil Rights Act of 1964 mandated that the workplace be free of harassment based on sex. Title IX requires that educational programs receiving federal funding be free of sexual harassment. Both these titled laws are anti-discrimination statutes. Title VII offers the following definitions of sexual harassment:

> Unwelcomed sexual advances, requests for sexual favors, and other verbal or physical conduct of a sexual nature when:

- Submission to such conduct by an individual is made explicitly or implicitly a term of employment;
- Submission to, or rejection of such conduct by an individual is used as the basis for an employment decision;
- And such conduct has the purpose or effect to interfere with an individual's work performance, or creates a hostile or intimidating environment.

The above definition concerns employment conditions; however, "education" can be substituted for "employment" in the definitions, and the basis for Title IX violations would be evident. Specifically, Title IX states: "No person in the United States shall, on the basis of sex, be excluded from participation in, be denied the benefits of, or be subjected to discrimination under any education program or activity receiving Federal financial assistance." While the amount of financial assistance necessary to trigger protection has not been established, most Catholic parishes or parish-sponsored programs have taken some government funds or services at some time and, thus, would be well-advised to comply with Title IX as far as possible. Courts, including the Supreme Court, are vigorously supporting persons' rights to be free from sexual harassment.

Thus, it would appear that if Title IX applies to the Catholic school, for example (and no case to date has held that it does not), students are protected against sexual harassment in much the same manner that employees are protected. Since religious education programs are sponsored by parishes in much the same manner as schools are sponsored, it seems that participants should be protected from sexual harassment. There have been reports of peer sexual harassment in religious education/youth ministry situations that have been reported to civil authorities.

SPECIFIC ACTIONS THAT CAN BE CONSTRUED AS HARASSMENT

The following are examples of behaviors that could constitute sexual harassment: sexual propositions, off-color jokes, inappropriate physical contact, innuendoes, sexual offers, looks, and gestures. In a number of recent public school cases, female students have alleged that male students made sexual statements to them and that school officials, after being informed, declined to take action, often accompanied by the remark, "Boys will be boys." The majority of these cases have been settled out of court, and money has been paid to the alleged victims.

Although one can argue that the *person* who sexually harasses another should be liable, and not the program and its administrators, case law is suggesting that supervisors who ignore such behavior or do not take it seriously can be held liable to the offended parties. (See *Jane Doe v. Special Sch. Dist. of St. Louis County,* 901 F.2d 642 [8th Cir. 1990].)

SUGGESTED POLICIES

One of the most important actions a pastor or other minister can take with regard to sexual harassment is to implement clear policies defining sexual harassment and detailing procedures for dealing with sexual harassment claims. The following is one suggestion of a policy statement:

Definition: Sexual harassment is defined as: (1) threatening to impose adverse employment or academic, disciplinary, or other sanctions on a person, unless favors are given; and/or (2) conduct, containing sexual matter or suggestions, which would be offensive to a reasonable person.

Sexual harassment includes, but is not limited to, the following behaviors:

(1) Verbal conduct such as epithets, derogatory jokes or comments, slurs, or unwanted sexual advances, imitations, or comments;
(2) Visual contact, such as derogatory and/or sexually-oriented posters, photography, cartoons, drawings, or gestures;
(3) Physical contact such as assault, unwanted touching,

blocking normal movements, or interfering with work, study, or play because of sex;

(4) Threats and demands to submit to sexual requests as a condition of continued employment or grades or other benefits or to avoid some other loss and/or offers of benefits in return for sexual favors; and

(5) Retaliation for having reported or threatened to report sexual harassment.

Procedures for Reporting should then be given. These procedures should include a statement such as, "All allegations will be taken seriously and promptly investigated." Confidentiality should be stressed. Concern should be expressed for both the alleged victim and the alleged perpetrator. Any forms that are to be used should be included in the procedures.

All catechists, youth ministers, teachers, other employees, and volunteers should be required to sign a statement that they have received a copy of the policies relating to sexual harassment and other sexual misconduct, have read the material, and agree to be bound by it. Parent/student handbooks should contain at least a general statement that sexual harassment is not condoned in a civilized atmosphere, let alone a Christian setting. Both parents and students should sign a statement that they agree to be governed by the handbook.

PREVENTION

It is far easier to prevent claims of sexual harassment than it is to defend them. To that end, employees, catechists, and volunteers should participate in some kind of inservice training that raises awareness of sexual harassment and other gender issues. Staff members must understand what sorts of behaviors can be construed as sexual harassment.

All staff members should discuss issues of fair treatment of others with those they supervise and should promptly correct any students who demean others. Defenses such as, "I was only kidding," will not be accepted if the alleged victim states that the behavior was offensive and unwelcome, and a court finds that a reasonable person could view the behavior offensive and unwelcome.

A recent incident will illustrate. During a religious education class, a boy and a girl approached the pencil sharpener. The boy stepped in front of the girl, sharpened his pencil, turned and blew the shavings on the girl's chest, and then swept his hand across the girl's sweater as he stated, "Here, let me help you get that off." The girl and her parents complained. The boy was verbally reprimanded, but was not punished nor was he required to apologize. A lawsuit was threatened. It was determined that the parish had a policy, the DRE was aware of it, but volunteer catechists had never been told of it. Although this case could very well have ended up in court, the parents declined to file the lawsuit.

Finally, of course, sexual harassment and other forms of demeaning behavior have no place in parishes or programs sponsored by parishes. Guarding the dignity of all members of the parish community should be a priority for all.

AIDS and Other Blood-borne Pathogens

The word "AIDS" evokes many emotions: fear, compassion, pity, and anxiety, to name a few. Today's ministers are no strangers to these emotions. It is not surprising that personnel have questions and concerns.

Some staff members believe that a person who is HIV-positive must report that status to the parish or program administrator. A number of court cases, however, protect the privacy rights of individuals. There would have to be some overwhelming, compelling reason for privacy rights to be violated. One example sometimes offered is the situation in which a student is prone to biting. Legal experts suggest that clear evidence must indicate that there is a history of this kind of behavior, not merely a fear that such behavior might occur.

Some administrators question whether a supervising adult has to become involved in a situation in which the blood of an individual known to be HIV-positive is involved. The standard which determines the duty in any situation involving young people is the *reasonable person* standard. The fact-finder in a court case must determine whether the staff member acted the way a reasonable person in the individual's position would act. For example, a teacher has a higher responsibility to students than a stranger would have to them. There is a good possibility that a judge or jury would not accept fear of coming in contact with blood as a reason for a teacher or other adult supervisor to decline trying to protect young people.

In the light of legal and ethical concerns, universal precautions should always be used when dealing with any situation involving body fluids. The prudent approach is to assume that everyone may be infected and to take universal precautions when dealing with body fluids. Every staff member should have gloves and disinfectant within easy access, and all parishes should offer inservice training in this area.

RECOMMENDATIONS

The following recommendations might provide a basis for discussion.

1. Remember that all people, including people with AIDS, are protected against discrimination.
2. Remember that everyone has privacy rights. Medical information is confidential and only those with a legal right to know can be informed.
3. Assume that any staff member or student may be HIV-positive or may have a communicable disease.
4. Do not discuss the physical, psychological, mental, or emotional condition of any person with anyone except professional staff (when necessary), parents, and/or those the parents designate.

5. Attitudes are important and can be expressed as much by actions as by words.
6. Teachers and other professionals are held to a higher standard than are "ordinary" people.

It should be clear that the law requires institutions to be non-discriminatory. The fear of AIDS is real. It is the task of parish personnel to model Christian behavior and values in this regard as it does in all others. The question that should always be asked is: What would Jesus do?

Parish Finances, the IRS, and Deductions

Perhaps no aspect of Catholic school administration is more troublesome than financial matters. Many of the problems associated with collection and reporting of tuition payments appear to center around Catholic schools. Even if the reader is not directly involved in a school situation, the principles discussed in this section could be helpful in other situations as well.

Principals spend much of their time budgeting, collecting tuition, attempting to raise money, and worrying about money. It can be very easy to forget that finances are larger than money considerations; civil law must also be considered when financial policies are developed and implemented.

CONTRACT LAW: THE BASIS FOR FINANCES

Contract law governs the operation of the Catholic schools and other programs. Parental or participant rights are determined by the provisions of the contract they have with the school or parish. Parents, teachers, and administrators must look to the contracting documents to determine the financial obligations of each party.

Since the administration and those who set policy for the

school or program determine the content of contracts, pastors and principals should ensure that contracts clearly state financial expectations, e.g., the amount of tuition charged, the possible payment arrangements, the penalties for delayed payments, etc. Carefully written documents that leave no room for misinterpretation are an administrator's best protection against allegations of unfairness and/or civil lawsuits.

The parent/student handbook constitutes a contract between the parent and the school or program. To protect everyone, parents should be required to sign a statement such as, "We have read this handbook and agree to be governed by it." Certainly, there is an assumption that a person who enrolls a child in a school or program is agreeing to the rules and regulations; that assumption, however, becomes fact when a written statement to that effect is on file in the school.

TUITION CONTRACTS

Many schools now require parents to sign separate tuition contracts or include all financial policies in the parent/student handbook. Tuition contracts provide evidence that a debt is owed to the school. In the 1987 case of *Thomas Jefferson School v. Kapros,* 728 S.W.2d 315, the court held that, according to its rules, a school could expel a student and that the parent could be required to pay the full year's tuition since the parent had signed a contract which bound him to the payment of liquidated damages if his child did not complete the school year.

Such a judgment may seem harsh, at first glance. Administrators, however, budget for expenses based on a certain number of students; if students withdraw, the expenses remain. As difficult as it may be, those responsible for Catholic schools must remember that the school, while primarily a ministry, is also a business, and bills must be paid. When purchasing an automobile, the buyer agrees to make monthly payments; if the person later decides the automobile isn't suitable, he or she is still bound to make the payments to the financier.

Principals and other policy makers should bear in mind that exceptions can always be made to a policy. For example, if a parent signs a tuition contract and is later transferred to another city, the principal should be able to make an exception and waive the payment of the remainder of the tuition. If, however, a student simply decides he or she would rather go to a different school, the principal may decide to hold the parents to the contract.

TITHING AS TUITION

A relatively recent practice of requiring parents to tithe or to make a contribution of a certain amount in the collection basket each week so that their children can attend the parish school poses special problems if those parents then take income tax deductions for those contributions. The Tax Code and Internal Revenue Service regulations do not allow the deduction of tuition from income tax. Thus, parishes who wish to use tithing as tuition should consult with diocesan attorneys to ensure that the parish is operating within existing law.

One approach to tithing might be to have a suggested minimum contribution for all parishioners. Any contributing parishioner would be entitled to participate in any and all parish programs, including the school. The issue is a complex one that cannot be adequately considered in this text. Pastors, principals, and boards, however, should be aware that there can be IRS ramifications when tuition is tied to contributions to the parish. At no time should a suggestion be made that parents can procure an education for their children, support the church, and earn a tax deduction for a charitable contribution.

BONDING PERSONS WHO HANDLE FINANCES

Parish administrators should seriously consider bonding individuals who handle money for the parish or school. Should an unfortunate situation occur and money be embezzled or otherwise misappropriated, the parish or school will be able to recover lost funds.

The topic of finances is a serious one. Careful planning, consultation with diocesan, parish, and/or school attorneys, and periodic review should help the parish and those who are responsible for its operations to keep it functioning in a financially and legally sound manner.

To Copy or Not to Copy?

Most administrators and ministers realize that copyright laws exist. If asked, many would probably respond that there are rules that should be followed when making copies of articles, book chapters, computer programs, and television broadcasts. Most people have seen notices on copy machines warning persons making copies that they are subject to the provisions of the copyright law.

REASONS TO COPY

In the 1960s and 1970s budgetary considerations were the reasons given by churches, including Catholic churches, that copied songs from copyrighted works and used the copies to compile parish hymnals. Courts have consistently struck down such uses and have ordered the offending churches to pay damages.

Today, church personnel appear to be aware of the legal consequences of copying and many subscribe to the licensing arrangements of music companies; for a given sum of money, the institution can make as many copies of music as desired during the span of the contract.

At the same time, it is not uncommon to find school teachers, religious educators, and youth ministers copying such items as workbooks, portions of textbooks, and other commercially published print materials. The swift advance of technology has catapulted computer programs, videocassettes, and similar media into the sphere of widespread copying.

COPYRIGHT LAW

Copyright law recognizes that authors and creators are entitled to the fruits of their labors; those who use an author's creations without paying royalties, buying copies, or seeking permission are guilty of stealing.

WHAT IS "FAIR USE"?

Section 107 of the 1976 Copyright Act deals with "fair use." It specifically states that the fair use of copies for teaching purposes "is not an infringement of copyright."

The sticking point is what the term "fair use" means. The section lists four factors to be included in any determination of fair use:

(1) the purpose and character of the use, including whether such use is of a commercial nature or is for nonprofit educational purposes;
(2) the nature of the copyrighted work;
(3) the amount and substantiality of the portion used in relation to the copyrighted work as a whole;
(4) the effect of the use upon the potential market for or value of the copyrighted work.

Educators and other ministers should have little or no trouble complying with the "purpose and character of the use" factor. Religious educators generally copy materials to aid the educational process. It should be noted, however, that recreational use of copied materials is generally not allowed under the statute.

"The nature of the copyrighted work" can prove a bit more problematic than "character and purpose." Who determines what is the nature of the work—the creator? the copyright holder? the teacher or minister? the judge or the jury? Almost any material can be classified as educational in some context; even a cartoon can be found to have some educational purpose if one is willing to look for it. It seems reasonable that, in determining "nature," a court would look to the ordinary use of the work and to the author's intent in creating it.

The "amount and substantiality" of the work copied is especially troublesome in the use of videocassettes and computer programs. Educators understand that they are not supposed to copy a whole book, but they may not understand that videotaping a television program or a movie or copying a computer program for student use can violate the "amount and substantiality" factor.

A relatively new practice, developing libraries of copies, is emerging in some schools and religious education programs. Whether the collections are of print materials or non-print materials, such as videotapes and computer programs, the practice of building collections can easily be subjected to scrutiny.

The last of the four factors, "effect on the market," is also difficult to apply in the educational setting. Arguments can be advanced that students would not rent or purchase commercially available items, even if the copies weren't available. It appears, though, that use of an author's work without appropriate payment for the privilege is a form of economic harm. Good faith generally will not operate as an acceptable defense in educational copyright or infringement cases.

COPYING GUIDELINES

A Congressional committee developed "Guidelines for Classroom Copying in Not-for-Profit Educational Institutions," printed in House Report 94–1476, 94th Congress 2d Sess. (1976). Pastors and other administrators should ensure that catechists have access to copies of the guidelines, which are readily available from local libraries, the Copyright Office, and members of Congress. Although these guidelines do not have the force of law that a statute has, judges do use them in deciding cases. Some examples of the guidelines follow.

For poetry, copying a complete poem of less than 250 words printed on no more than two pages, or copying an excerpt of 250 words from a longer poem is allowed. For prose, a complete work of less than 2,500 words or an excerpt from a longer work of not more than 1,000 words or 10% of the work is permissible. The guidelines mandate that copying meet this test of *brevity*.

The copying must be *spontaneous*. The educator must have decided more or less on the spur of the moment to use an item. Spontaneity presumes that a person did not have time to secure permission for use from the copyright holder. An individual who decides in September to use certain materials in December has ample time to seek permission. In such a situation, failure to seek permission means that the spontaneity requirement will not be met.

A last requirement is that the copying must not have a *cumulative effect*. Making copies of a number of poems by one author would have a cumulative effect in so far as collected works of the author would not be bought as a result.

Similarly, the practice of "librarying" is not permitted. Video-tapes may be kept for 45 days only. During the first 10 days, a teacher may use the tape once in a class (although there is a provision for one repetition for legitimate instructional review). For the remaining 35 days teachers may use the tape for evaluative purposes only.

Pastors, directors of religious education, and principals are responsible for supervision of all aspects of the educational process. If a catechist is charged with copyright violation, it is likely that the DRE will be charged as well. Clear policies and careful monitoring of those policies can lessen exposure to liability. As many legal authorities have observed, copyright violation is stealing. It appears, then, that "Thou shalt not steal" remains good law.

A Final Thought

At this point, readers may be overwhelmed at the scope and complexity of legal issues. One should always remember the words of Jesus when he was criticized for healing on the Sabbath when such activity did not seem to meet the "legal" requirements for Sabbath conduct: "The Sabbath was made for man, not man for the Sabbath" (Mk 2:27). The law is a parameter, but not a totality. The law protects all of ministry within its parameters. Awareness of the law enables a minister to act decisively and confidently. In the end, though, the question must always be, not "What can I do legally?" but, "Considering the legal options in responding to this situation, what would Jesus do?" Such a question focuses the minister and helps to ensure compliance both with Gospel imperatives and legal requirements.

Glossary

Board

A board (committee/council/commission) is a body whose members are selected or elected to participate in decision-making at the diocesan, regional, inter-parish, or parish level.

Collegiality

Collegiality is the sharing of responsibility and authority. In the Catholic Church, bishops have the highest authority within a diocese. Powers may be delegated to other parties, such as boards.

Common Law

Common law is that law not created by a legislature. It includes principles of action based on long-established standards of reasonable conduct and on court judgments affirming such standards. It is sometimes called "judge-made law."

Compelling State Interest

A compelling state interest is the serious need for governmental action. For example, the government is said to have a compelling state interest in anti-discrimination legislation and the equal treatment of all citizens.

Contract

A contract is an agreement between two parties. The essentials of a contract are: (1) mutual assent, (2) by legally competent parties,

(3) for consideration, (4) to subject matter that is legal, and (5) in a form of agreement that is legal.

Corporal Punishment

Corporal punishment is a type of punishment that involves the infliction of physical pain. Corporal punishment is any touching that can be construed as punitive.

Defamation

Defamation is communication that injures the reputation of another without just cause. Defamation can be either spoken (slander) or written (libel).

Due Process

Due process is fundamental fairness under the law. There are two types:

Substantive Due Process: "The constitutional guarantee that no person shall be arbitrarily deprived of his life, liberty or property; the essence of substantive due process is protection from arbitrary unreasonable action" (Black, p. 1281). Substantive due process involves *what* is done as distinguished from *how* it is done (procedural due process).

Procedural Due Process: How the process of depriving someone of something is carried out; *how it is done.* The minimum requirements of Constitutional due process are *notice* and a *hearing* before an *impartial tribunal.*

Fiduciary

A fiduciary is one who has accepted the responsibility for the care of people or property.

Foreseeability

Foreseeability is "the reasonable anticipation that harm or injury is the likely result of acts or omission" (Black, p. 584). It is not necessary that a person anticipate that a specific injury might result from an action, but only that danger or harm in general might result.

Invasion of Privacy

Invasion of privacy is a tort action in which the plaintiff alleges that the defendant has unreasonably invaded personal privacy, e.g., revealing confidential information in student or personal files without the individual's consent.

Judicial Restraint

Judicial restraint is the doctrine that courts will not interfere in decisions made by professionals.

Malpractice

Malpractice is a tort action in which the plaintiff alleges harm resulting from a professional's failure to act according to reasonable standards.

Negligence

Negligence is the absence of the degree of care which a reasonable person would be expected to use in a given situation.

Policy

A policy is a guide for discretionary action. Policy states *what* is to be done, not *how* it is to be done.

Proximate Cause

Proximate cause is a factor contributing to an injury. The injury was a result or reasonably foreseeable outcome of the action or inaction said to be the proximate cause of an injury.

State Action

State action is the presence of the government in an activity to such a degree that the activity may be considered to be that of the government.

Subsidiarity
Subsidiarity is the principle that problems should be solved at the lowest possible level. Thus, if there is a complaint against a teacher, the teacher ordinarily should be confronted before the principal is approached.

Tenure
Tenure is an expectation of continuing employment.
> ***De Facto* Tenure:** *De facto* tenure is an expectation in fact that employment will continue, in the absence of a formal tenure policy. *De facto* tenure can result from past practices of an employer or from length of employment.

Tort
A tort is a civil or private wrong as distinguished from a crime.

Bibliography

Black, Henry Campbell. *Black's Law Dictionary*, (1990), St. Paul: West.

Brooks v. Logan Joint District No. 2, 903 P.2d 73 (1995).

CACE/NABE Governance Task Force (1987). *A Primer on Educational Governance in the Catholic Church.* Washington, D.C.: NCEA.

Canon Law Society (1983). *The Code of Canon Law* (in English translation). London: Collins Liturgical Publications.

Dolter v. Wahlert, 483 F.Supp. 266 (N.D. Iowa 1980).

Geraci v. St. Xavier High School, 13 Ohio Op. 3d 146 (Ohio, 1978).

"Guidelines for Off-Air Recording of Broadcast Programming for Educational Purposes." Cong. Rec. E4750 (daily ed. October 14, 1981).

Jane Doe v. Special School District of St. Louis County, 901 F.2d 642 (8th Cir. 1990).

Reardon v. LeMoyne, 454 A.2d 428 (N.H. 1982).

Rendell-Baker v. Kohn, 102 S. Ct. 2764 (1982).

Smith v. Archbishop of St. Louis, 632 S.W.2d 516 (Mo. Ct. App. 1982).

Tinker v. Des Moines Independent School District, 393 U.S. 503 (1969).

Titus v. Lindberg, 228 A.2d 65 (N.J., 1967).

20 United States Code, Sec. 1232g, The Buckley Amendment, Family Education Rights and Privacy Act (1974).

United States Code Annotated.

Weithoff v. St. Veronica School, 210 N.W.2d 108 (Mich. 1973).